CYBERSECURITY

Cybersecurity Essentials:

Safeguarding Your Digital World

Alex Foster

TABLE OF CONTENTS

INTRODUCTION

The digital landscape is growing unprecedentedly in today's interconnected society, bringing incredible ease and evident threats. Technology has ingratiated itself into our lives, allowing us to interact, communicate, and transact in ways that were unthinkable just a few decades ago. Cyber threats, a fresh breed of threats brought on by the digital revolution, have the potential to compromise our personal data, financial security, and even the basic systems that keep our societies running.

Welcome to " Cybersecurity: Cybersecurity Essentials-Safeguarding Your Digital World." This e-book has been written to guide you through the maze of cyber risks, arming you with the information and resources required to move about the online world securely and confidently. This e-book is meant to empower you, whether you're an individual looking to safeguard your personal information, a professional trying to strengthen the security measures in place at your company, or just someone who wants to know more about the digital threats we face.

Understanding cybersecurity fundamentals is no longer optional in this digital age, where cyber attacks vary from sophisticated data breaches that target large companies to deceptive phishing emails that attempt to trick individuals. Our e-book will guide you through the key ideas, routines, and tactics that can protect you from the always-changing threats lurking in cyberspace.

In Chapter 1, we dive into the basics of cybersecurity; we'll build the framework for the rest of the e-book. What is cybersecurity, and why is it so important in the modern world? We'll dissect several cyberattacks in Chapter 2 as we examine the shadowy side of the digital world, drawing on historical precedent and understanding the motivations behind these attacks.

Your online presence is accessed through your digital identity, so Chapter 3 is all about securing it. We'll talk about the value of multi-factor authentication, the significance of strong passwords, and the precautions you can take to prevent your personal information from falling into the wrong hands. Additionally, Chapter 4 will equip you with the knowledge necessary to identify and resist phishing, a common threat.

Our e-book focuses on creating a virtual fortress rather than just protecting against attackers. While Chapter 6 discusses safe browsing techniques in the face of an abundance of potential threats, Chapter 5 walks you through protecting your devices and networks. Chapter 7 focuses on safeguarding your priceless digital assets with encryption and routine backups.

Chapter 8 discusses the human element of cybersecurity since it acknowledges that it is not just a technical issue. The realm of social engineering and manipulative techniques will be shown, emphasizing the value of awareness and knowledge. As we turn our attention to the business world, Chapter 9 explores corporations' particular difficulties and offers suggestions for creating effective cybersecurity policies.

The future is also covered in Chapter 10 of this e-book, where we'll talk about new threats and how modern technologies are influencing the cybersecurity environment. Chapter 11 looks into penetration testing and its function in uncovering vulnerabilities for individuals interested in ethical hacking.

"Cybersecurity: Cybersecurity Essentials- Safeguarding Your Digital World" is a call to action. It inspires you to cultivate a cybersecurity mindset, use caution while dealing with evolving security concerns, and take preventative measures to safeguard your online reputation. So, whether you're a digital novice or an experienced professional, I urge you to join me on this journey of empowerment as we work to protect our digital world and solve the complexities of cybersecurity.

CHAPTER I

Understanding Cybersecurity Basics

Definition of cybersecurity and its significance

The concept of "cybersecurity" has emerged as a crucial tenet of contemporary civilization in the quickly changing context of the digital age. Fundamentally, cybersecurity includes a wide range of methods, tools, and strategies to protect digital systems, networks, and data against expanding cyber threats. In this section, we will examine cybersecurity's broad definition and consider its enormous importance in today's linked world.

Cybersecurity includes a wide range of safeguards to prevent unauthorized access, attempts, and destruction of networks, systems, and data. These precautions are designed as a layered shield, with complex technology, protocols, and human interventions all working together to defend the digital world against various malevolent forces.

At its most basic level, cybersecurity focuses on preventing, identifying, and responding to cyber threats, ranging from ordinary viruses and malware to sophisticated hacking attempts. It involves a combination of preventative steps, such as installing firewalls and encryption, and reactive ones, including creating incident response and recovery plans. The definition of cybersecurity changes to reflect new technology and emerging threats as the digital ecosystem develops.

It is impossible to exaggerate the importance of cybersecurity in the modern world. Because of the profound integration of digital technologies into our lives, jobs, and societies, there is now an unprecedented level of connectivity and comfort. However, our interconnectedness makes us vulnerable to several threats that could significantly disrupt our lives.

The value of the data in the digital realm largely drives the importance of cybersecurity. Electronically stored personal data, financial information, intellectual property, and vital infrastructure systems are all potential targets for cybercriminals looking to steal information for financial gain, espionage, or even to cause chaos. Identity theft, financial loss, economic interruption, and weakened national security are all possible outcomes of a successful cyberattack.

Additionally, the "digital transformation," or the growing digitization of sectors of the economy and fundamental services, creates a variety of vulnerabilities in addition to new opportunities and conveniences. Nearly every industry now depends on interconnected digital systems, from power grids to healthcare systems, transportation networks, and manufacturing procedures. They serve as potential targets for cyberattacks because of their interconnectedness, which could have devastating consequences.

In recent years, the emergence of interconnected devices under the Internet of Things (IoT) banner has made the cybersecurity landscape even more difficult. Functionality and convenience, as opposed to strong security features, are frequently prioritized in the design of these devices, which range from smart home appliances to industrial sensors. Due to their lack of security, they are open to being taken advantage of by malicious actors, who can then utilize the compromised devices as gateways into more extensive networks.

In conclusion, cybersecurity is the guardian of our digital age. It protects our complex web of systems and data against a wide range of constantly changing threats. Its importance comes from our modern lives and societies being deeply connected to the digital world. Cybersecurity breaches can compromise sensitive information, disrupt daily life, and threaten national security.

As we continue to reap the rewards of innovation and digitization, we must give cybersecurity first priority. This calls for the use of innovative techniques and protocols as well as the promotion of a culture of knowledge and awareness. It takes a team effort from individuals to governments, businesses to educational institutions to create and maintain the strong defenses required to move about the digital world safely. The importance of cybersecurity is unwavering in a world where the next cyber threat is only a few clicks away, reminding us that the effectiveness of our cyber defenses will determine how the world uses technology in the future.

Types of cyber threats (malware, phishing, hacking, etc.)

In the sprawling landscape of the digital age, where technology is interwoven with every facet of modern life, the specter of cyber threats looms ominously. These threats, ranging from insidious malware to cunning phishing schemes and audacious hacking attempts, have become synonymous with the vulnerabilities inherent in our interconnected world. This section explores the diverse types of cyber threats, shedding light on their characteristics, impacts, and the imperative need to guard against them.

Malware, short for malicious software, represents a broad category of cyber threats designed to infiltrate, disrupt, or steal information from digital systems. Viruses, worms, Trojans, ransomware, and spyware are among its various forms. These digital assailants often rely on deceptive tactics to gain entry, exploiting vulnerabilities in software or human behavior. Once inside, they can cause havoc, from destroying data and crippling networks to holding critical information hostage until a ransom is paid. The advent of ransomware, in particular, has underscored the potentially crippling impact of malware, affecting individuals, businesses, and even healthcare institutions, highlighting the necessity of robust cybersecurity defenses.

Phishing, a form of social engineering, represents an artful manipulation of human psychology. Cybercriminals employ deceptive emails, messages, or websites that appear legitimate to induce recipients into divulging sensitive information, such as passwords, credit card details, or personal data. The ubiquity of phishing attacks is a testament to their effectiveness, as they exploit trust and familiarity to gain unauthorized access to individuals' digital lives. Whether through spear phishing, which targets specific individuals, or the more widespread mass phishing campaigns, these schemes prey on human vulnerabilities, making cybersecurity awareness and education essential in safeguarding against their pernicious impacts.

Hacking, the art of exploiting vulnerabilities in digital systems, is the most widely recognized form of cyber threat. Hackers, often operating with varying motivations, can infiltrate networks, systems, and databases to steal, manipulate, or compromise information. Ethical hackers, known as "white hat" hackers, use their skills to identify vulnerabilities and strengthen defenses, while malicious or "black hat" hackers pursue personal gain, activism, or even state-sponsored espionage. High-profile breaches of major corporations and government entities serve as stark reminders of the far-reaching consequences of hacking, including financial losses, reputational damage, and the potential exposure of sensitive information.

A planned assault on a digital service, network, or website with the goal of overwhelming its resources and blocking access to legitimate users, is known as Distributed Denial of Service attack. This is typically accomplished by saturating the target with an enormous amount of traffic, frequently produced by a compromised device network referred to as a "botnet." The motivations behind DDoS attacks can vary from financial gain through extortion to ideological statements or simple disruptions. DDoS assaults, in particular, have the potential to bring down online platforms, resulting in losses for companies and obstructing access to essential services, making their prevention and mitigation critical elements in cybersecurity strategies.

Insider threats occur when individuals with authorized access to a system or network misuse their privileges for malicious purposes. This category encompasses a range of scenarios, including disgruntled employees leaking sensitive information, contractors stealing proprietary data, or unwitting staff falling prey to social engineering schemes. Insider threats pose unique challenges as they exploit the trust and access granted to authorized personnel. Mitigating these threats demands a combination of technical measures, such as access controls and monitoring, along with a focus on organizational culture, training, and awareness.

The diverse array of cyber threats poses a formidable challenge in a world where digital technologies underpin nearly every aspect of modern life. Malware, phishing, hacking, DDoS attacks, and insider threats are among the most prevalent and disruptive forms of cyber attacks, exploiting specific vulnerabilities in digital systems and human behavior. The impact of these dangers can include everything from compromised personal and governmental security to monetary losses and reputational harm.

A multi-faceted approach to cybersecurity is imperative to counter this ever-evolving digital menace. Technical solutions, such as advanced antivirus software, firewalls, and encryption, provide the defense foundation. However, these measures must be supplemented by a strong emphasis on education and awareness. Human behavior must be made a crucial line of defense by ensuring that people and organizations have the knowledge to determine and respond to potential threats.

As cyber threats evolve in complexity and scale, pursuing cybersecurity becomes an ongoing endeavor. The collaboration of individuals, businesses, governments, and cybersecurity experts is essential in creating a resilient digital landscape. We can confidently navigate the digital age and make sure that the advantages of technology far outweigh the risks provided by the shadows of the virtual world by recognizing the intricacies of various cyber threats and adopting a holistic approach to security.

Common vulnerabilities in digital systems

In an era defined by the ubiquitous presence of digital systems, from personal devices to critical infrastructure, the vulnerabilities inherent in these systems have come to the forefront of our technological consciousness. As the digital landscape evolves astonishingly, so do the methods by which cybercriminals exploit weaknesses in these systems. This section delves into common vulnerabilities in digital systems, exploring their origins, manifestations, and the need to address them in the quest for a secure digital future.

Software, the foundation upon which digital systems are built, is often rife with vulnerabilities that malicious actors can exploit. Coding errors, known as "bugs," can create unintended pathways for cybercriminals to infiltrate systems. One of the most notorious forms of software vulnerability is the "zero-day exploit," wherein hackers target a vulnerability before it is publicly known, leaving software developers with zero days to fix it. This highlights the race between security professionals and hackers, as discovering and remedying vulnerabilities becomes a critical aspect of software development and system maintenance.

The failure to update software and apply security patches is a vulnerability that remains distressingly common. Many successful cyber attacks exploit known vulnerabilities that could have been prevented through timely updates. Hackers often target systems where security patches have not been applied, taking advantage of organizations' complacency. The notorious WannaCry ransomware attack of 2017, which affected thousands of systems worldwide, demonstrated the havoc that can be wreaked by exploiting unpatched vulnerabilities. This underscores the significance of regular updates as a fundamental defensive measure against potential threats.

Authentication and access control mechanisms form the gateways to digital systems. Weak passwords, lack of multi-factor authentication (MFA), and inadequate access controls create openings for unauthorized access. Credential stuffing attacks, where hackers use stolen credentials from other breaches to gain unauthorized access, highlight the importance of robust authentication practices. Equally important is making sure that users have the proper levels of access depending on their positions and responsibilities. Failure to implement strong authentication and access controls can lead to unauthorized data breaches, unauthorized system manipulation, and unauthorized entry into critical infrastructure systems.

One of the most insidious vulnerabilities in digital systems is the human factor. Social engineering exploits human psychology to manipulate individuals into divulging sensitive information or performing actions compromising security. Phishing, pretexting, and baiting are examples of social engineering tactics that target human vulnerability rather than technical weaknesses. Cybercriminals often capitalize on our willingness to trust and inclination to assist others. Educating individuals about these tactics and fostering a culture of skepticism are essential steps in mitigating the impact of this human vulnerability.

Encryption, a process of encoding data to prevent unauthorized access, is crucial to digital security. Insufficient or outdated encryption protocols can leave data vulnerable to interception, manipulation, and theft. Data breaches involving sensitive personal information or confidential business data can have far-reaching consequences, including identity theft and financial loss. The modern digital landscape demands the use of strong encryption to protect data both in transit (as it's transmitted between systems) and at rest (when it's stored on servers or devices).

In the intricate web of the digital world, the vulnerabilities that threaten our systems are diverse and ever-evolving. From coding errors to weak authentication practices, from unpatched software to social engineering tactics, these vulnerabilities expose us to the risk of cyber attacks that can have devastating consequences. Recognizing and addressing these vulnerabilities require a multi-faceted approach encompassing technological solutions and human awareness.

As technology advances, so too must our understanding of potential vulnerabilities and the implementation of strategies to mitigate them. Developers must prioritize secure coding practices and swift patch deployment. Users must be educated about the dangers of weak authentication and the perils of social engineering. Organizations must invest in regular security assessments, robust access controls, and encryption mechanisms. And as a society, we must acknowledge that maintaining digital security is a shared duty that calls for all of us to be vigilant.

In the digital age, where our lives are increasingly intertwined with technology, the vulnerabilities that lurk within our systems demand our unwavering attention. By addressing these vulnerabilities proactively and holistically, we can confidently navigate the complex landscape of digital systems, ensuring that the benefits of technology are harnessed while minimizing the risks that shadows of the digital realm pose.

CHAPTER II

Fundamentals of Cyber Attacks

In-depth exploration of different types of cyber attacks

In the intricate web of the digital age, where information flows seamlessly across vast networks, cyberspace has become a battlefield of sorts. Here, the adversary is often unseen, operating in the shadows with the intent to exploit vulnerabilities and compromise systems. These digital assailants deploy a diverse array of tactics known as cyber attacks, each tailored to exploit specific weaknesses within the complex architecture of the digital world. This section embarks on an in-depth exploration of various types of cyber attacks, shedding light on their methods, motivations, and the imperative need for robust defense strategies.

Cyber attacks encompass a broad spectrum of tactics with distinct characteristics and objectives. While these tactics vary widely, they all share the goal of gaining unauthorized access to systems, networks, or data. Some cyber attacks focus on causing immediate disruption, while others are subtler, aiming to extract sensitive information over time. Understanding the different categories of cyber attacks is crucial in recognizing the threat landscape and formulating effective defensive measures.

Malware attacks, as one of the most prevalent forms of cyber threats, come in various guises. Viruses attach themselves to legitimate programs, replicating and infecting other files when executed. Worms spread autonomously across networks, exploiting vulnerabilities and consuming resources. Trojans masquerade as benign software but contain malicious payloads that are unleashed once installed. Ransomware encrypts files and demands payment for their release. Spyware secretly gathers sensitive information. These attacks often rely on user actions, exploiting security lapses in software or exploiting human behavior, highlighting the importance of vigilant cybersecurity practices and user education.

Phishing attacks resemble digital sleight of hand because they use deception to trick users into disclosing sensitive information or taking security-compromising activities. Email phishing, a common variant, presents seemingly authentic messages that prompt users to click on malicious links or provide login credentials. Spear phishing narrows the focus to target specific individuals or organizations. Business Email Compromise (BEC) scams impersonate high-level executives to deceive employees into transferring funds. The success of phishing attacks often hinges on exploiting psychological triggers, demonstrating the need for user education and security awareness training to recognize and resist such tactics.

Hacking, the quintessential form of cyber attack, involves unauthorized entry into systems, networks, or devices intending to exploit or manipulate data. Ethical or "white hat" hackers employ their skills to identify vulnerabilities and enhance security. However, malicious or "black hat" hackers pursue various motives, from financial gain to activism or espionage. State-sponsored hacking involves nation-states targeting adversaries' systems for political or military advantage. Cyber espionage, a subcategory of hacking, focuses on stealing sensitive information from governments, corporations, or individuals. The multifaceted nature of hacking highlights the need for stringent security measures, including penetration testing, vulnerability management, and robust access controls.

Denial of Service, or DoS, and Distributed Denial of Service, or DDoS, attacks target the availability of digital resources. In a DoS attack, a single device overwhelms a network or system, rendering it inaccessible. DDoS attacks amplify the impact by employing multiple compromised devices to flood the target. Cybercriminals can leverage botnets, networks of infected devices, to orchestrate massive DDoS assaults. These attacks disrupt services, websites, or networks, causing financial losses, reputational damage, and user frustration. Effective mitigation strategies involve traffic filtering, capacity scaling, and collaborative efforts to trace and neutralize botnets.

Advanced Persistent Threats (APTs) are sophisticated, targeted attacks that often remain undetected for extended periods. APT actors, including state-sponsored groups or cybercriminal organizations, focus on long-term espionage or data theft. They employ meticulous planning, custom malware, and evasion techniques to infiltrate networks and exfiltrate sensitive information. APTs emphasize stealth, making detection challenging. Effective defense against APTs involves continuous monitoring, threat intelligence sharing, and security measures that extend beyond traditional network boundaries.

The world of cyber attacks is dynamic and ever-evolving, mirroring the rapid pace of technological progress. From the stealthy infiltration of malware to the calculated tactics of phishing and social engineering, from the direct assaults of hacking to the disruptive force of denial of service attacks, the spectrum of cyber threats underscores the need for comprehensive and adaptable defense strategies.

Defenders must remain vigilant, proactive, and informed as cyber attackers continuously refine their methods. Organizations and individuals alike must cultivate a cybersecurity mindset, embracing a multifaceted approach that includes technological solutions, user education, and a culture of security awareness. The digital realm is not a static battlefield but a dynamic arena where adversaries and defenders engage in an ongoing contest. By understanding the motives and tactics behind different types of cyber attacks, we can fortify our digital fortresses and navigate the evolving threat landscape with resilience and confidence.

Real-world examples of major cyber attacks and their impacts

Unprecedented convenience and connectivity levels brought about by the digital age have also exposed us to unprecedented risks. Major cyber attacks have become a grim reality, with cybercriminals employing sophisticated techniques to breach defenses, compromise systems, and exploit vulnerabilities. These attacks are not confined to the virtual world; their reverberations are felt in the physical realm, affecting individuals, organizations, and even entire nations. This section delves into real-world examples of major cyber attacks, exploring their methods, consequences, and the critical lessons they teach us about the evolving nature of cyber warfare.

Stuxnet, discovered in 2010, is a watershed moment in the history of cyber attacks. This highly sophisticated worm was designed to target Iran's nuclear program, specifically its uranium enrichment centrifuges. Stuxnet's designers employed multiple zero-day vulnerabilities to infiltrate air-gapped systems, demonstrating that even isolated networks were not immune to digital assaults. The worm exploited flaws in the Siemens industrial control systems used in the facility, causing centrifuges to spin out of control and ultimately sabotaging the nuclear program's progress. Stuxnet exemplified the power of cyber weapons, showcasing the potential to disrupt critical infrastructure through cyber means, blurring the lines between digital and physical warfare.

In 2017, the NotPetya ransomware attack wreaked havoc on a global scale. Disguised as ransomware, NotPetya was, in reality, a destructive wiper malware designed to destroy data irreversibly. While it masqueraded as a financially motivated ransomware attack, its true intention was to cause widespread disruption and chaos. The attack began with the compromise of a Ukrainian tax software company's update mechanism. The malicious update subsequently spread to other companies, causing a cascade of infections that affected critical infrastructure, multinational corporations, and government agencies. NotPetya's impact was felt far beyond its initial targets, leading to significant financial losses and operational disruptions for organizations worldwide, underscoring the importance of robust cybersecurity measures and incident response planning.

One of the major credit reporting companies in the world, Equifax, was the victim of a significant breach of data in 2017 that exposed the personal data of 147 million individuals. The company's website software had a vulnerability that wasn't promptly patched, which led to the breach. The exposed data included names, Social Security numbers, birth dates, and more, making affected individuals vulnerable to identity theft and fraud. The breach's fallout extended beyond personal impacts, as Equifax faced legal consequences and public outrage. The incident highlighted the critical importance of timely patch management, the secure handling of sensitive data, and transparency in disclosing breaches to affected parties.

In December 2020, the SolarWinds supply chain attack sent shockwaves through the cybersecurity community. Cyber attackers infiltrated SolarWinds, a software provider used by numerous government agencies and businesses, and inserted a backdoor into the company's software updates. This backdoor allowed the attackers to access the networks of SolarWinds' customers, including U.S. government agencies and major tech companies. The extent of the attack's impact is still being uncovered, but it has revealed the potential vulnerabilities in supply chain attacks, emphasizing the importance of security not just within an organization's own systems but throughout its entire ecosystem.

The real-world consequences of attacking essential infrastructure were made clear by the Colonial Pipeline ransomware assault in May 2021. A ransomware group known as DarkSide compromised Colonial Pipeline's systems, forcing the company to shut down its operations to prevent the spread of the malware. The pipeline's shutdown led to fuel shortages, price increases, and panic buying along the U.S. East Coast. This incident underscored the vulnerability of critical infrastructure to cyber attacks and highlighted the need for improved cybersecurity practices and coordination between public and private sectors.

These real-world examples of major cyber attacks provide stark reminders of the power and reach of modern cyber threats. From sophisticated nation-state operations to financially motivated attacks and accidental data exposures, the breadth and impact of cyber attacks are wide-ranging and multifaceted. They serve as cautionary tales, revealing vulnerabilities in systems, organizations, and societies, and urging us to remain vigilant and proactive in defending against emerging threats.

As cyber attackers refine their tactics and exploit new vulnerabilities, the imperative to bolster cybersecurity measures becomes even more pressing. These examples highlight the need for robust defense strategies, including regular software updates, vulnerability management, incident response planning, and collaborative efforts across sectors. The digital realm is an uncharted frontier where battles are fought not with swords and shields but with lines of code and algorithms. It is a realm where the consequences of failure extend far beyond the virtual domain, affecting the physical world's safety, stability, and prosperity. As we learn from the lessons of these significant cyber attacks, we must harness our collective knowledge and determination to fortify our digital defenses and navigate the evolving landscape with resilience and foresight.

Motivations behind cyber attacks (financial gain, espionage, activism)

In the intricate landscape of the digital realm, where ones and zeros weave the fabric of modern society, the motivations that drive cyber attacks are as diverse as the threats they pose. These attacks can have a variety of goals, each with its own set of circumstances and intentions, ranging from monetary gain to espionage and activism. This section delves into the complex web of motivations behind cyber attacks, shedding light on the multifaceted nature of these digital aggressions and the underlying factors that fuel them.

Financial gain is one of the most pervasive and tangible motivations driving cyber attacks. Cybercriminals, often caused by the allure of monetary rewards, employ various tactics to achieve their objectives. One common avenue is ransomware attacks, where attackers encrypt critical data and demand a ransom for its release. These attacks can target individuals, businesses, or even municipalities, exploiting the urgency to regain access to vital information. Financially motivated attacks can also involve credit card fraud, identity theft, and fraudulent online transactions. The profitability of these endeavors has given rise to a lucrative underground economy where stolen data is bought and sold with impunity. This motivation underscores the significance of bolstering cybersecurity measures and collaboration across industries to thwart the economic incentives driving cybercrime.

Long associated with cloak-and-dagger operations, espionage has found a new digital frontier. Nation-states and threat actors use cyber espionage to gather sensitive information from governments, corporations, and individuals. The motivations behind cyber espionage can be political, economic, or military. Nation-states often employ cyber means to gain insights into adversaries' strategies, steal intellectual property, and acquire classified information. On the other hand, corporate espionage involves the theft of proprietary data to gain a competitive advantage or undermine rivals. The interconnected nature of the global economy and the digitization of sensitive information have made cyber espionage an attractive and potent tool for those seeking to gain the upper hand in the complex theater of international relations and commerce.

In the age of digital activism, the internet has become a battleground for social, political, and ideological causes. Hacktivists leverage cyber attacks to amplify their voices and enact change. These actors often target organizations or governments they perceive as oppressive, corrupt, or conflicting with their values. Distributed Denial of Service, or DDoS attacks, website defacements, and data leaks are common tactics hacktivists use to disrupt operations, spread awareness, or expose perceived wrongdoings. The motivations behind hacktivism are as diverse as the causes they champion, ranging from advocating for free speech to environmental conservation and human rights. While hacktivism can spark meaningful conversations and drive social change, its methods often blur ethical lines and raise questions about the legality and ethics of cyber attacks as a means of activism.

The motivations driving state-sponsored cyber attacks are deeply intertwined with geopolitics and national interests. Governments deploy cyber operations as tools of influence, control, and coercion. These attacks can take the form of economic espionage to gain financial advantage, political interference to shape public opinion, or sabotage to disrupt adversaries' capabilities. The Stuxnet attack, allegedly orchestrated by the United States and Israel against Iran's nuclear program, exemplifies the intricacies of state-sponsored cyber operations. These attacks often blur the lines between traditional warfare and cyber warfare, raising questions about international norms, rules of engagement, and the potential for escalation in the digital realm.

The motivations behind cyber attacks are as diverse as the individuals, groups, and nations that carry them out. From the pursuit of financial gain to the secrecy of espionage and the enthusiasm of activism, these motivations profoundly shape the digital landscape. As technology advances and our dependence on digital systems deepens, understanding these motivations becomes vital in shaping effective defense strategies and responses to cyber threats.

In addressing cyber attacks, a multifaceted approach is essential. Legal frameworks, international agreements, and ethical considerations must evolve to govern the complex realm of cyber operations. Governments, industries, and individuals must collaborate to bolster cybersecurity measures, share threat intelligence, and respond effectively to cyber attacks driven by various motivations. The digital age demands a new level of vigilance, where the motivations behind cyber attacks are decoded and countered with agility and resilience, ensuring that the promise of the digital era is not overshadowed by the threats that lurk within its code.

CHAPTER III

Securing Your Digital Identity

Importance of strong passwords and password management

In the intricate tapestry of the digital age, where our lives are interwoven with technology, passwords serve as the first line of defense against cyber threats. They act as digital keys, granting access to personal accounts, sensitive information, and valuable digital assets. Yet, despite their critical role, the importance of strong passwords and effective password management is often underestimated. This section delves into the significance of crafting robust passwords and adopting sound password management practices, shedding light on their role in fortifying our digital identities and safeguarding our virtual realms.

A strong password is a fortress, constructed with an intricate combination of characters that is difficult to predict or guess. It comprises a blend of uppercase and lowercase letters, numbers, symbols, and is of sufficient length to thwart automated hacking tools. Complexity is a formidable barrier against brute-force attacks, where attackers systematically attempt various combinations to crack passwords. A strong password, such as "P@ssw0rd#123," becomes exponentially more challenging to breach than a weak one, like "password123." The foundation of strong passwords rests on their complexity, rendering them resistant to the arsenal of techniques employed by cybercriminals.

Cybercriminals employ various tactics to exploit password vulnerabilities, including the dictionary attack. This technique involves using a pre-compiled list of words, names, or common phrases to attempt to crack a password systematically. Weak passwords, often derived from easily guessable terms like "123456," "qwerty," or "password," succumb to dictionary attacks swiftly. By crafting passwords that deviate from recognizable words and incorporate a mix of characters, users can thwart dictionary attacks and bolster their digital defenses.

Password reuse poses a grave threat to digital security, yet it remains a common and dangerous practice. Reusing passwords across multiple accounts magnifies the consequences of a breach in one area, as cybercriminals can access other accounts where the same password is employed. For instance, the compromise of an email account can serve as a gateway to financial accounts, social media profiles, and more. This domino effect underscores the importance of using unique passwords for each account, ensuring that a breach in one does not cascade into a chain of vulnerabilities.

Two-factor authentication (2FA) enhances the security of passwords by introducing an additional layer of verification. This method requires users to provide a second piece of information, often a temporary code sent to a mobile device, after entering their password. Even if a cybercriminal gains access to a password, 2FA acts as a barrier, as they would need physical possession of the second factor to breach the account. This effective method lessens the impact of password theft and adds a further level of protection against unauthorized access.

As the number of online accounts proliferates, managing passwords becomes increasingly daunting. Effective password management strategies alleviate this burden and enhance security. Password managers, secure applications that store and auto-fill passwords, offer a centralized solution. These tools generate and manage complex passwords for various accounts, ensuring strong security and convenience. Adopting passphrase techniques, where a sequence of unrelated words or a memorable sentence is used as a password, can balance complexity and memorability.

The importance of strong passwords and effective password management in digital security cannot be overstated. Passwords are guardians of our online identities, granting access to a myriad of services and sensitive information. Their strength lies in their complexity, uniqueness, and careful management. By crafting strong passwords, guarding against dictionary attacks, eschewing password reuse, embracing two-factor authentication, and adopting effective password management practices, individuals can forge digital armor that thwarts the ambitions of cyber criminals.

The digital age is a landscape brimming with opportunities and risks. As we navigate this terrain, the strength of our passwords becomes symbolic of our commitment to safeguarding our virtual identities and personal data. By recognizing the critical role of strong passwords and implementing sound password management strategies, we fortify the gates of the digital world, ensuring that our online journeys are marked by security, resilience, and the freedom to explore without fear.

Multi-factor authentication (MFA) and its role in identity protection

In the interconnected landscape of the digital age, where personal and sensitive information is exchanged across virtual domains, the need for robust identity protection has never been more pronounced. The advent of Multi-Factor Authentication (MFA) is a beacon of hope as traditional security measures continue to fall short in the face of rising cyber threats. MFA, a mechanism that combines multiple layers of verification before granting access, has emerged as a pivotal solution in the battle to secure digital identities. This section delves into the significance of Multi-Factor Authentication, exploring its principles, methods, and the transformative role it plays in safeguarding our virtual selves from the perils of the digital realm.

At its core, Multi-Factor Authentication (MFA) is a strategy that requires users to present two or more distinct forms of verification before gaining access to an account, system, or application. Unlike traditional single-factor authentication, which often relies solely on passwords, MFA introduces an additional layer of security. This supplementary factor could encompass something the user knows (password), something the user has (a smartphone or token), or something the user is (biometric data like fingerprints or facial recognition). By combining these factors, MFA adds complexity to the authentication process, creating a formidable barrier against unauthorized access.

MFA's strength lies in its ability to layer multiple forms of authentication, creating a holistic approach to identity protection. Even if a malicious actor obtains a user's password through hacking, phishing, or other means, MFA serves as a second line of defense. This layered approach reduces the impact of password breaches, as the attacker would need access to an additional factor (such as a smartphone or biometric data) to breach the account successfully. Consequently, MFA curtails the effectiveness of standard hacking techniques like brute-force attacks and credential stuffing.

Two-factor authentication, or 2FA, is a subset of multi-factor authentication (MFA) that has gained widespread adoption due to its ease of use and effectiveness. It requires users to provide two authentication factors, often combining something they know (password) with something they have (a verification code sent to their phone). However, MFA can incorporate more than just two factors. Three-factor authentication (3FA) or even higher iterations can include biometric data as a third factor, further elevating security. MFA's flexibility allows organizations and individuals to tailor their authentication methods to the sensitivity of the data and the risk profile of the environment.

Biometric authentication, a prominent element of MFA, relies on unique physical or behavioral characteristics to verify identity. Fingerprint scans, facial recognition, iris scans, and voice recognition are biometric factors used in authentication processes. Biometrics offer a compelling advantage because they are difficult to replicate and inherently tied to the individual. However, concerns about privacy, data security, and potential breaches of biometric databases underscore the need for stringent safeguards and regulatory oversight.

The ever-evolving landscape of cyber threats demands innovative solutions, and MFA has risen to the challenge. Phishing attacks, which often exploit the vulnerabilities of single-factor authentication, are rendered less effective against MFA-protected accounts. The attacker still requires the second factor to access the account, even if a user falls for a phishing scam and discloses their password. Similarly, credential stuffing attacks, where attackers use leaked credentials from other breaches, face a considerable hurdle in MFA-protected environments.

While the advantages of Multi-Factor Authentication are substantial, user experience and implementation challenges exist. The usability of MFA can influence its adoption, as some methods (like text messages or physical tokens) can be less convenient than others. Balancing security with user convenience is essential to ensure that MFA remains an accessible and effective solution. MFA must be integrated into various platforms and services, and users must be aware of its advantages if MFA is to be widely adopted.

As the digital landscape expands, so do the threats that lurk within it. Cybercriminals employ sophisticated tactics to breach defenses, compromise identities, and exploit vulnerabilities. In this context,

Multi-Factor Authentication emerges as a beacon of hope, reshaping the battle against cyber threats. By combining multiple layers of verification, MFA fortifies digital boundaries and empowers individuals and organizations to navigate the digital realm with confidence.

In embracing MFA, we transcend the limitations of passwords and embark on a journey toward a more secure digital future. However, MFA's efficacy hinges on its adoption and continuous evolution. To ensure that individuals as well as organizations can fully utilize MFA, it is crucial to strike the delicate balance between security and usability. As we venture further into the interconnected horizon of the digital age, Multi-Factor Authentication stands as a beacon, illuminating the path toward a safer, more resilient digital world.

Safeguarding personal information online (social media, public records)

In the digital age, where our lives are intricately interwoven with technology, preserving personal privacy has become an ever-elusive endeavor. The virtual realm, marked by the ubiquity of social media and the accessibility of public records, poses a dual challenge: it provides platforms for self-expression and connection while simultaneously exposing our personal information to a global audience. Safeguarding personal information online has become imperative, demanding vigilance, awareness, and strategic measures. This section delves into the complex landscape of online personal data, exploring the nuances of social media use, the implications of public records, and the strategies essential to protecting our digital identities and maintaining our privacy.

Social media, a ubiquitous facet of modern life, offers platforms for individuals to share thoughts, experiences, and moments with friends, family, and the wider world. Yet, this sharing comes with a trade-off: exposing personal information to a potentially vast and unknown audience. Each status update, photo, and location check-in contributes to a digital footprint that, when assembled, forms a comprehensive mosaic of an individual's life. While enhancing social connections, this mosaic can inadvertently provide malicious actors with insights that compromise personal privacy. Striking a balance between self-expression and safeguarding sensitive information is paramount in the quest for online privacy.

Oversharing on social media platforms poses one of the most significant threats to personal privacy. Posting detailed personal information, such as addresses, phone numbers, and travel plans, can provide cybercriminals with essential tools for identity theft, scams, and targeted attacks. Moreover, seemingly innocuous information like pet names or birth dates can serve as answers to security questions, enabling unauthorized access to accounts. Cybercriminals often exploit oversharing to craft convincing phishing emails or conduct social engineering attacks, underscoring the importance of restraint in sharing personal details online.

Beyond social media, personal information can also be gleaned from public records. Public records encompass many documents, such as property records, court filings, birth and death certificates, and more.

While these records serve legitimate purposes, their accessibility raises privacy concerns. Information extracted from public records can be used to build profiles, conduct background checks, or orchestrate sophisticated phishing attacks. The digital trail left by public records underscores the need for individuals to understand what information is accessible and to consider the potential implications of sharing personal details in various contexts.

Data aggregators, entities that compile and sell personal information from various sources, amplify the impact of public records. These entities mine online and offline data to create comprehensive profiles that include demographic data, browsing history, and purchase behavior. Aggregating seemingly disparate pieces of information paints a remarkably detailed picture of an individual's life. Data aggregators' commodification of personal data raises ethical concerns about consent and data ownership, highlighting the urgency of enacting strong data privacy regulations and advocating for individual rights over personal information.

Safeguarding personal information online demands a proactive approach encompassing awareness, education, and strategic measures. First and foremost, individuals must be mindful of the information they share on social media platforms, exercising caution when revealing personal details and considering the potential ramifications. Privacy settings should be configured to limit the visibility of posts and personal information to trusted connections. Furthermore, regularly reviewing and adjusting privacy settings is essential as platforms evolve.

Engaging in data minimization, the practice of sharing only necessary information is another pivotal strategy. Questioning the necessity of revealing specific details, such as birth dates or addresses, can prevent cybercriminals from accessing valuable data. Utilizing strong, unique passwords and enabling multi-factor authentication (MFA) on all accounts provides additional protection, reducing the risk of unauthorized access.

The cultivation of digital literacy plays a crucial role in safeguarding personal information. Educating oneself about online privacy risks, recognizing phishing attempts, and understanding the implications of public records can empower individuals to make informed decisions. Regularly monitoring online presence, conducting web searches to identify personal information, and opting out of data collection wherever possible contribute to maintaining a semblance of privacy in the digital age.

The challenge of safeguarding personal information online is an intricate dance between connectivity and privacy. Social media and public records offer unparalleled avenues for self-expression and information access but expose individuals to various privacy risks. Striking a balance between leveraging these tools and protecting personal data is essential to navigate the digital landscape safely.

As technology evolves, so must our strategies for preserving personal privacy. By adopting a proactive approach involving responsible social media use, data minimization, digital literacy, and strategic measures like strong passwords and MFA, individuals can reclaim control over their online identities. The quest for online privacy is a dynamic journey that requires ongoing vigilance and a commitment to safeguarding the digital aspects of our lives while embracing the benefits of the interconnected world.

CHAPTER IV

Navigating the World of Phishing

Understanding phishing attacks and their variations

In the intricate landscape of the digital realm, where information flows ceaselessly across virtual networks, a sinister threat looms—one that preys on human psychology, exploits trust, and capitalizes on the ubiquity of online communication. Phishing attacks, a devious form of cybercrime, have emerged as one of the most pervasive and insidious threats in the digital age. These assaults entail the skillful use of deceptive methods to trick individuals into disclosing sensitive information, like passwords, credit card information, or personal identification. This section delves into the multifaceted world of phishing attacks, exploring their methods, variations, and the crucial measures needed to thwart their ambitions and protect the integrity of the digital landscape.

At the heart of a phishing attack lies a devious subterfuge—a cunning attempt to impersonate legitimate entities, deceive recipients, and induce them into divulging confidential information. The term "phishing" derives from "fishing," as cybercriminals cast their digital nets wide, hoping to trap victims. These attackers craft emails, messages, or websites that mimic trusted sources, often impersonating banks, social media platforms, government agencies, or well-known brands. These forged communications deploy a mix of emotional triggers, urgency, and psychological manipulation to evoke a response, leading recipients to unwittingly provide sensitive information.

In a classic phishing attack, a fraudulent email leads the target to a fake website where they are asked to enter personal information. The email often creates a sense of urgency, implying dire consequences if the recipient fails to take immediate action. Whether it's a notice of a compromised account, a fake invoice, or a seemingly innocuous request for an information update, these attacks induce panic or curiosity to lure individuals into the trap. The fake website, which is made to look like the real one, tries to gather private data that can be used for fraud or other illegal activities.

Spear phishing elevates the art of deception to a more sophisticated level. In this variation, attackers customize their messages to target specific individuals or organizations. The attacker gathers information from publicly available sources, such as social media profiles, to tailor the message to the recipient's interests, affiliations, or work responsibilities. The familiarity of the message content and the appearance of legitimacy make spear phishing even more potent. Executives, employees with financial authority, and high-profile individuals are often targeted due to their potential for yielding valuable information or financial gain.

Whaling attacks are a subset of spear phishing that focuses on targeting the highest echelons of an organization—executives, CEOs, or other high-ranking officials. These attacks exploit their positions of power and access to sensitive information. Cybercriminals aim to trick these individuals into revealing confidential data or authorizing fraudulent financial transactions. Whaling attacks are meticulously planned, often involving in-depth reconnaissance and social engineering tactics. As organizations become increasingly aware of the risk, raising awareness and implementing robust security measures become paramount to thwarting whaling attacks.

Clone phishing capitalizes on previously legitimate email communications to instill false trust in recipients. In this tactic, attackers duplicate a genuine email, modify its contents slightly, and resend it to the original recipient. The modified email often contains a malicious link or attachment, which, when interacted with, can lead to malware infection or compromise sensitive information. Clone phishing leverages the recipient's familiarity with the sender and the content, making it a highly effective form of attack that preys on unsuspecting recipients.

While traditional phishing often involves email communication, cybercriminals have expanded their reach to other communication channels. Vishing, or voice phishing, involves attackers impersonating legitimate organizations through phone calls to extract sensitive information or financial details from the victim. Similarly, smishing, or SMS phishing, uses text messages to deceive recipients into disclosing information or clicking on malicious links.

These variations exploit trust in communication channels beyond email and demonstrate the evolving tactics of cybercriminals.

The battle against phishing attacks is one of perpetual vigilance and constant adaptation. As attackers refine their tactics and exploit new vulnerabilities, individuals and organizations must remain proactive in safeguarding their digital identities. Education emerges as a potent weapon against phishing attacks. Raising awareness about the various forms of phishing, recognizing common red flags, and promoting skepticism toward unsolicited requests can empower individuals to discern legitimate communication from fraudulent attempts.

Implementing robust security measures is equally critical. Secure email gateways can filter out malicious messages, while strong spam filters reduce the likelihood of phishing emails reaching recipients' inboxes. Multi-factor authentication (MFA) serves as a significant line of defense, adding an extra layer of security to account access. Organizations can conduct regular security awareness training to keep employees informed about emerging threats and evolving tactics, cultivating a culture of cybersecurity.

In the intricate ecosystem of the digital realm, phishing attacks are a ceaseless tide of deception. As cybercriminals continue to hone their tactics and leverage psychology to exploit human vulnerability, the battle for cybersecurity rages on. By understanding the various forms of phishing attacks, recognizing the hallmarks of deception, and embracing a multifaceted approach to defense, individuals and organizations can fortify their digital boundaries and navigate the deceptive seas with resilience and foresight. The light of awareness and the shield of knowledge stand as our staunchest allies in the always changing world of cyberthreats.

Recognizing common phishing tactics and red flags

In the intricate tapestry of the digital age, where communication and commerce intertwine across virtual realms, a sinister threat persists—one that preys on human psychology, exploits trust, and capitalizes on the ubiquity of online interactions. Phishing attacks, a pervasive form of cybercrime, have evolved into a complex ecosystem of tactics designed to deceive individuals and organizations. Recognizing these tactics and the telltale red flags they bear is essential in navigating the treacherous waters of the digital landscape. This section delves into common phishing tactics and their associated red flags, empowering individuals to unmask digital deception, fortify their defenses, and safeguard their digital identities.

Email spoofing is a classic tactic phishing perpetrators employ to manipulate the recipient's perception of the sender's identity. In order to make it seem as though the email is coming from a reliable source, attackers use this technique to forge the sender's email address. Recipients may receive messages seemingly from banks, service providers, or well-known brands, urging them to take immediate action. Red flags often include sender email address variations, subtle misspellings, or unusual domains. Paying meticulous attention to email addresses and headers can help recipients identify the telltale signs of email spoofing and avoid falling victim to impersonation attempts.

Phishing attacks often play on human psychology, invoking a sense of urgency or fear to elicit rapid responses. Attackers create scenarios that demand immediate action, such as account compromise, unauthorized transactions, or impending consequences if action is not taken. The language used in such emails may be excessively urgent or threatening. Red flags include phrases that induce panic, overly aggressive language, or demands for immediate payment or personal information. A healthy dose of skepticism toward unsolicited urgent requests is essential in thwarting these manipulative tactics.

Phishing attacks frequently employ links to direct recipients to fake websites or malicious downloads. These links often appear legitimate at first glance but lead to counterfeit websites designed to steal credentials or spread malware. Hovering over links to reveal the actual URL destination and examining the URL structure for anomalies can help users identify fraudulent links. Similarly, email attachments may contain malware or ransomware, seeking to compromise systems upon interaction. Caution must be exercised when encountering unexpected attachments, especially from unknown senders.

Phishing emails often lack the personalization characteristic of legitimate communication. Attackers use generic greetings like "Dear User" or "Valued Customer" to mask their lack of knowledge about the recipient. Poor grammar, spelling errors, and awkward sentence structures can also indicate inauthentic communication. Legitimate organizations typically invest in professional communication, making errors in language and presenting red flags for recipients to recognize.

Phishing attackers frequently lure recipients with promises of extravagant rewards, discounts, or prizes. These offers are designed to pique curiosity and entice recipients to click links or reveal personal information. If an offer seems too good to be true, it likely is. Red flags include requests for payment in exchange for a supposed reward, requests for personal information, and offers that promise disproportionate benefits.

Phishing attacks may leverage the illusion of trust by impersonating authority figures within organizations, such as CEOs or managers. These emails may instruct recipients to share sensitive information or make financial transactions under the pretext of following company protocols. These manipulative attempts can be detected by confirming the authenticity of such requests through alternate communication channels, such phone calls or in-person contacts.

Recognizing common phishing tactics and their associated red flags empowers individuals and organizations to defend against cyber threats proactively. Educating users about these tactics, fostering a culture of skepticism toward unsolicited requests, and conducting regular cybersecurity awareness training can equip individuals with the tools needed to detect and thwart phishing attempts. Employing email filters, anti-phishing software, and browser security extensions can also defend against malicious links and attachments.

In the ever-evolving realm of digital deception, vigilance is paramount. Encouraging open lines of communication within organizations and promoting a sense of responsibility for cybersecurity can further enhance the collective defense against phishing attacks. By fostering a comprehensive understanding of common phishing tactics and their red flags, individuals and organizations can unmask the art of digital deception, fortify their defenses, and ensure that the digital landscape remains a place of trust, integrity, and security.

Techniques to avoid falling victim to phishing scams

In the sprawling expanse of the digital realm, where communication and commerce intertwine seamlessly, a shadowy adversary lurks— phishing scams. As the digital landscape evolves, so do the tactics of cybercriminals who seek to exploit human psychology, manipulate trust, and compromise sensitive information. Falling victim to phishing scams can have dire consequences, from financial loss to identity theft. However, armed with knowledge and strategic techniques, individuals and organizations can navigate the deceptive seas safely and thwart the ambitions of these digital deceivers. This section delves into the multifaceted methods that empower individuals to avoid falling prey to phishing scams, fostering a culture of skepticism, vigilance, and informed decision-making.

The cornerstone of defense against phishing scams is cultivating a healthy dose of skepticism. Individuals should approach unsolicited emails, messages, or requests with a critical eye, questioning their authenticity. Cybercriminals often employ urgency and emotional triggers to manipulate recipients into hasty actions. Adopting an approach of "trust, but verify" can prevent rash decisions driven by emotional appeals. Recipients must evaluate the communication's source, context, and content before taking action, especially if the request involves sharing personal information, clicking links, or making financial transactions.

A fundamental technique to avoid phishing scams is verifying the source of communication through independent and trusted channels. If an email requests sensitive information, financial transactions, or unusual actions, recipients should reach out to the alleged sender using contact information from official sources—such as official websites, phone directories, or previously saved contact information. By sidestepping the links or contact details provided in the suspicious communication and instead initiating contact through established channels, individuals can confirm the legitimacy of the request and avoid potential traps.

Links in phishing emails may appear legitimate but lead to fraudulent websites designed to steal sensitive information or distribute malware. Hovering the mouse pointer over a link without clicking on it can reveal hidden intentions. This reveals the actual destination URL, which might differ from the text displayed in the email. By scrutinizing the URL structure and assessing its alignment with the sender's claimed identity, recipients can gauge the credibility of the link and avoid being misled.

Attachments in phishing emails often harbor malware or malicious scripts that compromise the recipient's device upon interaction. A crucial technique is to exercise caution when encountering unexpected attachments, especially if the email's content feels unusual or suspicious. Instead of opening the attachment directly, individuals should scan it with reliable antivirus software or share it with their IT department for assessment. This practice shields against inadvertently triggering malware and reinforces a defensive posture against phishing attacks.

Individuals should employ secure browsing practices when interacting with websites that require sensitive information. Look for "https://" at the beginning of the website's URL and the padlock icon in the address bar. This indicates that the connection is encrypted, safeguarding data from interception by malicious actors. When inputting sensitive data into online forms, like passwords or credit card details, secure browsing is crucial.

Enabling Multi-Factor Authentication (MFA) adds an extra layer of defense against phishing attacks. Even if a cybercriminal obtains login credentials, they still need the additional factor—a code sent to a trusted device—to access the account. MFA reinforces security by minimizing the impact of compromised passwords and serves as an effective deterrent against unauthorized access.

Education is a potent tool in the fight against phishing scams. Organizations and individuals should invest in regular cybersecurity awareness training to empower users with the knowledge to recognize and respond to phishing attempts. Training sessions can cover the latest phishing tactics, red flags, and practical techniques to safeguard against deception. Organizations can develop a cooperative defense against cyber threats by providing individuals with the knowledge to recognize and report phishing attempts.

Proactive measures are the compass that directs individuals as well as organizations to safety in the digital age, when phishing scams thrive in the shadows of virtual environments. By cultivating a culture of skepticism, verifying sources through independent communication channels, exercising caution with attachments and links, practicing secure browsing, and embracing multi-factor authentication, individuals can navigate the deceptive seas of the digital world with confidence. Regular cybersecurity education is a beacon of knowledge, illuminating the path toward informed decision-making and resilience against evolving phishing tactics.

As technology evolves and cybercriminals adapt their approaches, the techniques to avoid falling victim to phishing scams must also evolve. Armed with vigilance, awareness, and a commitment to cybersecurity, individuals can stand as formidable bulwarks against digital deception. The seas may be treacherous, but with strategic techniques and a steadfast dedication to defense, individuals can navigate safely and secure their digital identities and assets from the lurking threat of phishing scams.

CHAPTER V

Fortifying Your
Devices and Networks

Securing your computer and mobile devices

In the expansive realm of the digital age, where our lives intertwine seamlessly with technology, the security of our computers and mobile devices stands as an imperative fortress against the onslaught of cyber threats. These devices are gateways to our digital identities, sensitive information, and virtual realms. Yet, the evolving landscape of cybercrime necessitates a proactive approach to fortify these gateways against intrusions. This section delves into the multifaceted domain of securing computers and mobile devices, exploring robust strategies, best practices, and cutting-edge techniques essential to safeguarding our digital fortresses and maintaining the sanctity of our digital spaces.

The foundation of securing computers and mobile devices lies in installing antivirus and antimalware software. These tools act as the first line of defense against many threats, ranging from viruses and worms to Trojans and ransomware. Regularly updating these programs ensures they remain equipped to detect and neutralize the latest forms of malware. The efficacy of these tools hinges on their comprehensive database of threat signatures and heuristic analysis, allowing them to identify suspicious patterns and behaviors that could indicate malware infiltration.

Firewalls serve as digital perimeters, controlling incoming and outgoing traffic to and from a device. A software firewall, often integrated into operating systems, monitors and filters network activity to prevent unauthorized access. Hardware firewalls, such as those integrated into routers, add a further layer of protection by filtering traffic before it reaches the device. Enabling firewalls at the software or hardware level is a fundamental technique to thwart unauthorized intrusion attempts and safeguard against malicious network activity.

Software developers frequently release updates to patch vulnerabilities and address security flaws. Ignoring these updates exposes computers and mobile devices to exploitation by cybercriminals who target known weaknesses. An unpatched software vulnerability was to blame for the data breach at Equifax in 2017, which exposed the personal information of millions of individuals. Users can close potential entry points that cybercriminals might exploit by regularly updating operating systems, applications, and plugins.

The strength of passwords cannot be overstated. Using complex passwords comprising a mix of uppercase and lowercase letters, numbers, and symbols creates a formidable barrier against unauthorized access. Implementing unique passwords for each account minimizes the damage in case of a breach. Additionally, augmenting passwords with Multi-Factor Authentication (MFA) introduces an extra layer of protection. After entering their password, MFA requires users to provide a second piece of information, often a temporary code sent to a mobile device. Even if attackers acquire a password, they still need physical possession of the second factor to breach the account.

Data encryption serves as a shield for sensitive information, both at rest and in transit. Encrypting data at rest involves scrambling information stored on devices to prevent unauthorized access if the device is lost or stolen. Encryption in transit safeguards data exchanged between devices by encoding it, preventing interception by malicious actors. Using secure protocols like HTTPS when browsing and accessing online services enhances protection by ensuring encrypted data transmitted between devices and servers.

Application whitelisting involves allowing only approved applications to run on a device, minimizing the risk of malicious software execution. Similarly, following the least privilege principle limits user and application access to only the necessary resources and permissions. This reduces the attack surface and prevents cybercriminals' potential exploitation of elevated privileges. Implementing application whitelisting and adhering to the least privilege principle enhances security by narrowing the pathways through which threats can infiltrate a device.

Devastating consequences may result from data loss brought on by malware, hardware failure, or other unforeseen circumstances.

Important data is protected from loss and disruption by routinely being backed up to external storage devices or cloud services. Backup solutions should be automated, encrypted, and tested periodically to ensure data integrity. Backups offer a safety net against ransomware attacks, allowing users to restore their systems to a state before the attack occurred.

Securing Wi-Fi networks is crucial to prevent unauthorized access and eavesdropping. Users should change default router passwords, employ strong Wi-Fi encryption protocols (WPA3 is currently recommended), and disable remote administration. Security is further improved by renaming the network's SSID to a nondescript name and turning on network isolation, which prohibits devices connected to the same network from talking with one another. Public Wi-Fi networks should be used sparingly and only when encrypted connections, such as VPNs, are established to protect data from interception.

Securing computers and mobile devices is an ongoing endeavor. Regular security audits involve evaluating the effectiveness of security measures, identifying potential vulnerabilities, and adapting strategies to evolving threats. Simultaneously, user training is essential to equip individuals with the knowledge to recognize and respond to security risks. Organizations should provide comprehensive cybersecurity awareness training, informing users about emerging threats, safe practices, and strategies to mitigate risks.

In the sprawling seas of the digital landscape, securing computers and mobile devices is a voyage of perpetual vigilance and proactive defense. Cyber threats evolve quickly, challenging individuals and organizations to adapt and fortify their digital fortresses. By installing and updating security software, enabling firewalls, maintaining regular software updates, implementing strong passwords and MFA, encrypting data, practicing application whitelisting and the least privilege principle, backing up data, and following secure Wi-Fi practices, individuals can anchor themselves in a safe digital haven.

Securing computers and mobile devices requires harmoniously orchestrating techniques and best practices, each vital in creating a layered defense against cyber threats. As technology evolves, so must our approach to cybersecurity. By embracing these techniques, individuals and organizations can confidently navigate the ever-changing tides of the digital realm, knowing that their digital fortresses stand resilient against the relentless waves of cyber adversity.

Importance of software updates and patches

In the intricate tapestry of the digital age, where technology permeates every facet of our lives, the security and stability of our digital landscapes stand as paramount concerns. Software, the backbone of modern computing, is the conduit through which our devices communicate, transact, and store information. Yet, this intricate ecosystem is not immune to vulnerabilities that cybercriminals eagerly exploit. The significance of software updates and patches, often overlooked or delayed, cannot be overstated. This section delves into the multifaceted importance of software updates and patches, exploring their role in bolstering security, enhancing functionality, and fortifying the foundations of our digital world.

Software vulnerabilities represent the chinks in the digital armor that cybercriminals quickly exploit. The cybersecurity landscape is rife with attackers targeting known vulnerabilities to infiltrate systems, exfiltrate sensitive information, or propagate malware. Software updates and patches, released by developers in response to identified vulnerabilities, serve as the first line of defense against such attacks. These updates shore up weaknesses in the code, closing the doors that malicious actors seek to pry open. Failing to apply updates promptly is akin to leaving the front door of a fortress unlocked, inviting cybercriminals to exploit the exposed vulnerabilities.

Zero-day vulnerabilities pose a particularly ominous threat. These are vulnerabilities that are exploited by cybercriminals before software developers have the chance to release patches. In a race against the clock, cyber defenders must swiftly develop and distribute patches to mitigate the threat. Zero-day exploits can lead to catastrophic breaches, as demonstrated by the Equifax data breach in 2017. Millions of people's personal data were compromised as a result of the attackers' usage of a vulnerability in the widely used web application framework Apache Struts. The incident underscored the urgency of effectively-staying abreast of software updates and patches to counter zero-day vulnerabilities.

Software updates and patches are not solely about security; they also play a pivotal role in enhancing functionality and performance. Developers release updates to introduce new features, improve user experiences, and optimize performance. These updates reflect the ongoing evolution of technology, incorporating user feedback and emerging trends. Delaying updates leaves systems vulnerable and denies users access to improved features and functionality. By embracing updates, users can unlock many benefits beyond security, enriching their digital experiences.

Software updates ensure compatibility and interoperability in the intricate web of interconnected devices and applications. Updates often address compatibility issues arising from operating systems, hardware, or other software component changes. Failing to update can lead to outdated software incompatibility with newer systems, rendering devices or applications dysfunctional. This can disrupt operations, impede collaboration, and lead to inefficiencies in the corporate environment. Regularly applying updates ensures that devices and software remain synchronized with the evolving digital ecosystem.

In many industries, adherence to regulatory standards and compliance requirements is non-negotiable. Software updates often include patches addressing compliance-related issues, ensuring organizations meet legal obligations and industry standards. Neglecting these updates can lead to legal liabilities, financial penalties, and reputational damage. The General Data Protection Regulation, which was established by the European Union, is one such instance. Organizations that handle personal data are legally bound to protect it, and failure to apply updates that address security vulnerabilities can result in severe consequences.

In the interconnected digital world, individuals and organizations are responsible for safeguarding personal and business data. Cyberthreats, which include ransomware attacks and data breaches, compromise sensitive information, halt operations, and damage reputations. Applying software updates and patches is a fundamental practice that contributes to this shared responsibility. Individuals can ensure that their personal devices are fortified against cyber threats, while organizations can create a resilient security posture that safeguards customer data and preserves trust.

Software updates and patches are an investment in cyber resilience—a strategy that prepares systems to withstand and recover from cyber attacks. Just as individuals maintain their physical health through preventive measures like exercise and a balanced diet, digital systems require consistent upkeep through updates. Cybercriminals constantly innovate, exploiting new vulnerabilities and techniques. Regularly applying updates ensures that systems remain equipped to fend off emerging threats. By proactively future-proofing devices and software, individuals and organizations fortify their defenses and reduce the potential impact of cyber incidents.

Managing software updates and patches requires a strategic approach that balances security, functionality, and efficiency. Organizations should implement patch management policies prioritizing critical security updates while considering the impact on operations. Tools for automated patch management help speed up the procedure and guarantee that updates are applied quickly and consistently on all systems. Individuals should enable automatic updates whenever possible and establish a routine to check for updates manually. These strategies ensure that the task of managing updates remains manageable and effective.

The importance of software updates and patches cannot be overstated in a digital landscape teeming with opportunities and vulnerabilities. These updates constitute a collective effort in cyber hygiene, shaping a secure and resilient digital environment. By mitigating security vulnerabilities, enhancing functionality, ensuring compatibility, and upholding legal obligations, software updates serve as the linchpin that holds the digital realm together. As technology evolves, so must our commitment to applying updates—a commitment that bolsters security, fortifies resilience, and paves the way for a safer and more interconnected future.

Configuring firewalls and antivirus software

In the complex tapestry of the digital realm, where our lives intertwine seamlessly with technology, protecting our digital assets and personal information is an imperative task. Amidst the ever-evolving landscape of cyber threats, configuring firewalls and antivirus software is critical in building strong digital defenses. These tools act as sentinels, guarding the gates of our digital domains against unauthorized access and malicious intrusions. This section delves into the multifaceted field of configuring firewalls and antivirus software, exploring their significance in cybersecurity, the principles that underpin their effectiveness, and the strategies that empower users to establish robust digital fortifications.

Hardware and software-based firewalls serve as the first line of defense against cyber threats. Operating at the network level, a firewall monitors and controls incoming and outgoing traffic, enforcing predefined rules that determine whether data packets are allowed to pass through or are blocked. Configuring firewalls involves establishing these rules, creating a digital perimeter that shields devices and networks from unauthorized access. This configuration can be customized to allow or block specific ports, applications, or IP addresses, effectively mitigating potential entry points for cybercriminals.

Firewalls offer dual protection through inbound and outbound filtering. Inbound protection scrutinizes incoming traffic to ensure that only legitimate and safe data reaches the network or device. On the other hand, outbound protection examines outgoing data to prevent unauthorized transmissions of sensitive information. This holistic approach safeguards against external threats seeking entry and prevents data exfiltration by malicious software or actors. Configuring firewalls to enact robust inbound and outbound filtering is essential for a comprehensive defense strategy.

Application firewalls, a subset of firewalls, provide a layer of application-specific protection. Unlike traditional firewalls that operate based on network ports and protocols, application firewalls scrutinize the behavior of individual applications. By monitoring the actions of applications and allowing only authorized behaviors, application firewalls counteract attacks that exploit vulnerabilities in specific software. For instance, web application firewalls (WAFs) focus on protecting web applications from attacks like SQL injection and cross-site scripting. Configuring application firewalls ensures that the unique security needs of various applications are met with precision.

Antivirus or anti-malware software is a digital sentinel that scans for and removes malicious software, or malware, from devices. Configuring antivirus software involves selecting scan types, scheduling scans, and updating malware databases to detect the latest threats. Antivirus software employs signature-based detection, comparing files to known malware signatures, and heuristic analysis, identifying suspicious behavior patterns. These techniques work in tandem to identify and neutralize a wide range of malware, from viruses and worms to Trojans and ransomware.

Antivirus software employs two primary scanning methods: real-time scanning and on-demand scans. Real-time scanning continuously monitors files, downloads, and programs as they are accessed or executed, identifying and quarantining threats in real time. On-demand scans are manually initiated scans that scrutinize specific files, folders, or the entire system for malware. Configuring antivirus software to perform both real-time scanning and regular on-demand scans ensures a balanced approach, providing ongoing protection and the flexibility to assess specific areas for potential threats.

Configuring firewalls and antivirus software involves enabling automatic updates and scheduled scans. Automatic updates ensure that the software's databases of known threats are up to date, allowing them to identify and neutralize the latest malware. Scheduled scans, on the other hand, automate the process of scanning devices at predefined intervals, reducing the need for manual intervention. Regularly scheduled scans complement real-time protection by proactively identifying and removing any dormant or previously undetected threats.

While the primary purpose of firewalls and antivirus software is to identify and neutralize threats, there are instances where specific files, applications, or processes are incorrectly flagged as malicious due to false positives. Configuring exclusions allows users to specify files, folders, or applications that should be excluded from scans or firewall rules. This fine-tuning ensures that legitimate software and processes are not disrupted or misidentified as threats, enhancing the software's accuracy and usability.

Configuring firewalls and antivirus software is most effective when integrated with safe browsing practices. Users should be cautious when clicking links, downloading files, or interacting with unknown websites. The software acts as a safety net, but users play a crucial role in preventing the initiation of potential threats. Similarly, secure Wi-Fi practices and regular software updates complement the protective capabilities of firewalls and antivirus software, creating a holistic defense strategy.

In the rapidly evolving digital landscape, configuring firewalls and antivirus software constitutes a unified front against various cyber threats. By establishing digital perimeters through firewalls and harnessing the threat-detection capabilities of antivirus software, users erect formidable defenses that safeguard sensitive information, personal data, and digital experiences. Configuration involves aligning the software with specific needs, balancing real-time protection and scheduled scans, and fine-tuning security measures to accommodate legitimate software. As the digital realm continues to evolve, configuring firewalls and antivirus software remains pivotal—an ongoing commitment to protecting the integrity of our digital world.

CHAPTER VI

Safe Browsing Practices

Choosing secure web browsers

In the vast expanse of the digital frontier, where our lives are intricately woven with technology, web browsers serve as the vessels that carry us across the virtual landscapes. They are our windows to the internet, connecting us to information, communication, and a world of online possibilities. However, the digital realm is not without its perils, and choosing a web browser carries significant implications for our online security and privacy. This section delves into the multifaceted landscape of choosing secure web browsers, exploring the criteria that define browser security, the vulnerabilities that threaten our digital experiences, and the strategies that empower users to navigate the digital frontier safely.

Security lies at the heart of the browser selection process. Web browsers that are secure are protected from a variety of online risks, such as malware, phishing scams, data breaches, and intrusive tracking. They employ encryption to safeguard data exchanged between the user and websites, shielding sensitive information from interception by malicious actors. Additionally, secure browsers integrate robust security features, such as anti-tracking tools, pop-up blockers, and automatic updates, to proactively defend against evolving threats.

A critical criterion for a secure web browser is its commitment to regular security updates. In the dynamic landscape of cybersecurity, vulnerabilities are identified and exploited at an alarming rate. Browser developers release updates to patch these vulnerabilities and strengthen their defenses. Choosing a browser that promptly and consistently issues security updates ensures that users remain protected against the latest threats. A prime example is the Spectre and Meltdown vulnerabilities discovered in 2018, which exposed many processors to potential attacks. Browsers that rapidly incorporated mitigations via updates demonstrated their commitment to user security.

Privacy is another crucial dimension of secure web browsing. Privacy-oriented browsers prioritize shielding users from invasive data collection practices, often by blocking third-party cookies, trackers, and advertisements. They offer enhanced privacy modes that prevent websites from tracking users across sessions and browsing history from being retained. These features are vital in an age where user data is commodified and exploited for targeted advertising, surveillance, and monetization.

Secure web browsers empower users with control over their security and privacy settings. They offer customizable options to enable or disable features such as location tracking, JavaScript execution, and plugin functionality. These settings allow users to tailor their browsing experience to their needs and risk tolerance. By providing granular control, browsers ensure that users can balance security, functionality, and convenience.

A secure web browser integrates anti-phishing and malware protection mechanisms that warn users about potentially malicious websites and downloads. These features rely on real-time databases of known threats and heuristic analysis to identify suspicious patterns. The browser displays warning messages that prevent interaction when a user tries to enter a website that has been identified as phishing or containing malware. These safeguards are instrumental in preventing users from falling victim to cybercriminal tactics.

While security and privacy are paramount, the compatibility and performance of a web browser also factor into the decision-making process. A secure browser should be compatible with many websites and web applications, ensuring a seamless browsing experience. Similarly, it should be optimized for speed and responsiveness to avoid hindrances in productivity. Striking a balance between security, privacy, compatibility, and performance is essential to ensure that the chosen browser meets users' diverse needs.

Secure web browsers often support a variety of extensions and add-ons that enhance security and privacy. These tools include ad blockers, password managers, VPNs (Virtual Private Networks), and script blockers. Browser extensions extend the browser's functionality and allow users to customize their security posture. They can fortify defenses against ads that carry malicious code, manage passwords securely, and provide anonymity through encrypted connections.

Open source browsers, whose source code is publicly available, offer transparency that contributes to their trustworthiness. The open nature of the code allows independent experts to scrutinize it for vulnerabilities and backdoors. Browsers like Mozilla Firefox and Chromium (the open-source project behind Google Chrome) benefit from the collective efforts of a global community, fostering a culture of security and accountability.

Even with the most secure browser, user education and vigilance remain paramount. Users must be cautious when clicking links, downloading files, and sharing personal information. Phishing attacks and social engineering tactics often bypass technical defenses by exploiting human psychology. Regular cybersecurity awareness training and a healthy dose of skepticism toward unsolicited requests are essential in fortifying personal security.

In the boundless expanse of the digital frontier, the choice of a secure web browser is a decision that reverberates across our online experiences. The browser we choose shapes our interactions, safeguards our data, and determines our exposure to cyber threats. Individuals can confidently navigate the digital landscape by prioritizing security, valuing privacy, staying informed about vulnerabilities, and embracing user-controlled settings. Just as explorers choose sturdy vessels to cross treacherous waters, users can choose secure web browsers as their companions on the journey through the intricate realms of the internet—a journey defined by protection, empowerment, and the pursuit of a safer digital future.

Identifying secure websites (HTTPS) and avoiding malicious sites

In the vast and interconnected landscape of the internet, where information and interactions converge seamlessly, the security of our digital interactions is paramount. The distinction between secure and malicious websites holds profound implications for our online experiences—ranging from safeguarding personal information to mitigating cyber threats. This section delves into the intricate world of identifying secure websites through the HTTPS protocol and avoiding malicious sites, exploring the significance of secure connections, the vulnerabilities posed by malicious websites, and the strategies that empower users to navigate the web with confidence and caution.

The Hypertext Transfer Protocol Secure (HTTPS) is at the heart of secure web connections. This cryptographic protocol encrypts data exchanged between a user's device and a website, shielding it from eavesdropping and tampering by malicious actors. The padlock icon and also the "https://" prefix in the website's URL highlight the incorporation of HTTPS and reassure users that their connection is encrypted. When sending sensitive data like passwords, credit card information, and personal information, encryption is essential. HTTPS is an emblem of trust and transparency, ensuring that users' interactions with websites remain private and protected.

Unencrypted connections, symbolized by the HTTP protocol, pose substantial risks to users' security and privacy. In HTTP connections, data is transmitted in plain text, rendering it susceptible to interception by attackers lurking on the network. This vulnerability exposes users to various threats, including man-in-the-middle attacks, where attackers intercept and modify the communication between users and websites. Cybercriminals can exploit these vulnerabilities to steal sensitive information, inject malicious code, and perpetrate identity theft. Adopting HTTPS is a potent countermeasure that bolsters the integrity of online communications and reduces the surface area for potential attacks.

The foundation of the HTTPS protocol is provided by SSL (Secure Sockets Layer) and TLS (Transport Layer Security) certificates. These digital certificates are used as electronic credentials to verify a website's legitimacy and are distributed by Certificate Authorities (CAs). When users access a website with an SSL/TLS certificate, their browser performs a handshake, verifying the certificate's legitimacy. Using this procedure, the risk of phishing attacks that make use of domain impersonation is reduced because a secure connection is established and it is confirmed that consumers are engaging with the intended website.

The shift to HTTPS has become a cybersecurity imperative for all websites, transcending the realm of e-commerce and sensitive transactions. Major browsers have actively encouraged HTTPS adoption by flagging HTTP sites as "Not Secure" in the address bar. This visual indicator alerts users to the absence of encryption, fostering awareness about the security implications of their online interactions. Consequently, websites of all types, including blogs, informational sites, and online forums, are adopting HTTPS to ensure user confidence and protect their data.

While secure connections fortify online interactions, malicious websites lurk in the shadows, exploiting human psychology and technological vulnerabilities. Malicious websites encompass a spectrum of threats, from phishing sites that mimic legitimate platforms to malware distribution sites that disseminate harmful software. Social engineering tactics, like urgent notifications or emotional appeals, manipulate users into interacting with these sites. As technology evolves, attackers innovate new techniques, like drive-by downloads, where malware is injected into users' systems without their knowledge, illustrating the dynamic nature of the threat landscape.

Recognizing the red flags of malicious websites is pivotal in steering clear of potential dangers. Users should scrutinize URLs for inconsistencies, misspellings, and variations from the legitimate domain. Typosquatting, where attackers register domains similar to popular sites, is a common tactic to deceive users. Users should also be aware of unsolicited messages or emails that request personal information from them in exchange for links, files, or downloads. Hovering over links without clicking and carefully evaluating the authenticity of requests can prevent users from inadvertently interacting with malicious content.

Phishing websites, a prevalent form of online deception, mirror legitimate platforms intending to steal sensitive information. These sites often replicate the appearance of trusted entities, such as banks, social media platforms, and e-commerce sites. Unsuspecting users are enticed to enter their credentials, which attackers subsequently harvest. Vigilance in checking URLs, examining the website's design and layout, and being cautious of unsolicited requests for sensitive information are crucial in evading phishing websites' clutches.

Safe browsing practices serve as an armor against malicious sites and deceptive tactics. Users should navigate directly to websites by typing the URL or using bookmarks rather than relying on links from unknown sources. Implementing ad blockers and script blockers can thwart malicious ads and drive-by downloads. Moreover, web browser extensions that provide reputation-based site ratings and flag potentially harmful sites contribute to safer online interactions. Combining these practices augments users' ability to detect and evade malicious websites.

Empowering users to identify secure websites and avoid malicious ones hinges on cybersecurity education and awareness. Individuals should educate themselves about common cybercriminal tactics, stay informed about emerging threats, and continuously learn about secure online practices. Organizations should conduct regular cybersecurity training sessions to sensitize employees to the nuances of web security and equip them with the skills needed to navigate the web safely.

In the ever-evolving landscape of the digital frontier, identifying secure websites and avoiding malicious ones is a skill that transcends technology—a practice of vigilance, critical thinking, and empowerment. Adopting HTTPS, driven by SSL/TLS certificates, creates a foundation of secure connections that protect users' data and privacy. Simultaneously, a keen awareness of malicious websites, their tactics, and the strategies to evade their snares fortify users against the allure of deception. As users traverse the intricate web of the internet, armed with knowledge, mindfulness, and safe browsing practices, they embark on a safer digital odyssey—an expedition marked by secure interactions, guarded identities, and the preservation of the digital realm's sanctity.

Risks of public Wi-Fi and how to use it safely

In the interconnected landscape of the digital age, public Wi-Fi has emerged as a ubiquitous convenience that empowers users to remain connected anytime, anywhere. Whether in coffee shops, airports, hotels, or shopping malls, public Wi-Fi networks offer a gateway to the online world, enabling us to browse, communicate, and transact on the go. However, beneath the veneer of convenience lies a landscape fraught with risks that can compromise our security and privacy. This section delves into the multifaceted risks of public Wi-Fi networks and explores strategies to harness their convenience safely. By understanding the vulnerabilities inherent in these networks and adopting secure practices, users can navigate the wireless wilderness with confidence and caution.

Public Wi-Fi networks present an enticing proposition: free and accessible internet connectivity. However, the very attributes that make these networks attractive—ubiquity, convenience, and zero cost—are the ones that make them a breeding ground for cyber threats. Unlike secured private networks, public Wi-Fi networks are often open and lack encryption, rendering data transmitted over these networks vulnerable to malicious actors' interference. This vulnerability exposes users to various risks, including eavesdropping, data theft, and man-in-the-middle attacks.

In an open Wi-Fi environment, attackers can employ eavesdropping and packet sniffing techniques to intercept unencrypted data transmitted between users' devices and websites. This data can include login credentials, personal information, and even sensitive financial data. Cybercriminals equipped with readily available tools can exploit these vulnerabilities to collect valuable information, compromising users' privacy and security.

Man-in-the-middle (MITM) attacks are a potent threat in public Wi-Fi networks. In an MITM attack, the attacker places oneself in between the user and the target, intercepting and perhaps changing the data that is sent between them. Users interact with what they believe is a legitimate website or service, unaware that an adversary is manipulating their communication. This technique allows attackers to steal login credentials, inject malicious code, and manipulate transactions—a sobering reminder that even routine online activities can be compromised.

Cybercriminals often set up rogue Wi-Fi networks that mimic legitimate public hotspots. These networks, known as fake hotspots or evil twin networks, bear names similar to those of reputable establishments. Unsuspecting users connect to these networks, believing them to be legitimate, and unwittingly expose their data to attackers. By exploiting this trust, attackers can launch attacks such as credential theft, malware distribution, and phishing campaigns.

Unsecured public Wi-Fi networks lack encryption, making data transmission susceptible to interception. Attackers can monitor network traffic and collect unencrypted data, potentially compromising sensitive information. Users are exposed to identity theft, monetary fraud, and illegal access to personal accounts due to the absence of encryption.

While public Wi-Fi networks come with inherent risks, adopting safe practices can mitigate these vulnerabilities and allow users to leverage the convenience of these networks without compromising their security.

Whenever possible, opt for websites that use the HTTPS protocol. Websites using HTTPS encrypt data exchanged between users and the website, safeguarding it from interception by attackers. The use of HTTPS is denoted by the padlock icon in the browser's address bar. Additionally, consider using browser extensions that force HTTPS connections for websites that support it, ensuring a secure browsing experience.

By encrypting all data transferred between the user's device and the VPN server, virtual private networks (VPNs) add an additional degree of protection. This encrypted tunnel shields data from prying eyes on public networks. By connecting to a VPN server, users can browse the internet as if they were on a private network, reducing the risks associated with public Wi-Fi networks.

To prevent individuals on the network from accessing your files and data, disable sharing on your device. Furthermore, turn off auto-connect features that automatically connect to open Wi-Fi networks. This precaution prevents your device from inadvertently connecting to malicious or unauthorized networks.

Enabling two-factor authentication (2FA) on accounts adds an extra layer of security. Even if attackers are successful in obtaining login credentials, they would still require a second factor to access the account, which is frequently a temporary code transmitted to your phone. Even if your credentials are stolen over a network that is not secure, 2FA greatly minimizes the risk of illegal access.

Refrain from performing sensitive activities on public Wi-Fi networks, such as online banking, shopping, and accessing confidential accounts. These activities involve transmitting sensitive information that attackers could intercept. If such activities are unavoidable, consider using a VPN or a mobile data connection.

Ensure that your device's firewall is enabled to prevent unauthorized access. Additionally, have security software, including antivirus and antimalware tools, active and up to date. These layers of defense can detect and mitigate potential threats that may arise from using public Wi-Fi networks.

Use separate accounts for online activities that involve sensitive information. For instance, consider using a dedicated email account for financial transactions and critical communications. This practice limits the potential impact of a breach on other online accounts.

As the digital world increasingly intersects with our daily lives, public Wi-Fi networks offer an invaluable bridge between us and the online realm. However, this bridge also exposes us to risks that demand vigilance and precaution. By recognizing the vulnerabilities of public Wi-Fi networks and adopting secure practices, users can harness the convenience of wireless connectivity without compromising their security and privacy. From using encrypted connections and employing VPNs to turning off sharing settings and limiting sensitive activities, each step reflects an informed effort to confidently navigate the wireless wilderness—a journey marked by secure interactions, safeguarded data, and preserving our digital well-being.

CHAPTER VII

Protecting Your Digital Assets

Safeguarding sensitive files and data

Protecting sensitive files and data becomes a crucial duty in the vast digital world, where our lives are becoming evermore intertwined with technology. Our digital repositories hold a wealth of personal, financial, and confidential information, making them attractive targets for cybercriminals seeking to exploit vulnerabilities for financial gain or malicious intent. This section delves into the intricate domain of safeguarding sensitive files and data, exploring the significance of data security, the vulnerabilities that threaten our digital assets, and the strategies that empower users to fortify their digital vaults against cyber threats.

Data security is the linchpin that upholds the integrity of the digital ecosystem. Our files and data encompass a spectrum of information—ranging from personal photos and emails to financial records and proprietary business data. Breaches of this information can lead to identity theft, financial loss, reputational damage, and even compromise national security. The digital age has ushered in unprecedented conveniences, but it has also brought forth many cyber threats that exploit weaknesses in the fabric of our digital existence. As a result, safeguarding sensitive files and data is a pivotal responsibility that transcends individual interests—protecting the digital world's collective security and stability.

Cybercriminals employ a variety of tactics to breach digital defenses and access sensitive files and data. Malware, including viruses, worms, and ransomware, can infiltrate systems through deceptive links, infected email attachments, or compromised software. Phishing attacks manipulate users into disclosing login credentials, personal information, or financial details through seemingly legitimate communications. Insecure Wi-Fi networks, weak passwords, and unencrypted connections allow attackers to intercept data transmissions. Insider threats, either malicious or unintentional, can expose sensitive information from within organizations. Understanding these vulnerabilities is paramount in devising strategies to safeguard data against potential breaches.

Encryption is a powerful shield that protects sensitive files and data from unauthorized access. Data that has been encrypted becomes unreadable and can only be deciphered by utilizing a decryption key. This method guarantees that even if an attacker accesses encrypted data, they will be unable to decipher it without the right key. End-to-end encryption, which secures data from the sender to the recipient, is crucial in protecting data during transmission, particularly for sensitive communications and financial transactions.

Secure backup and recovery mechanisms are essential components of data security. Regularly backing up sensitive files to offsite or cloud storage ensures that data remains accessible even in device loss, theft, or hardware failure. However, the backup process should be approached with security in mind. Encryption should be applied to backup files, and access to backup storage should be restricted to authorized users. Similar to this, testing recovery processes on a regular basis guarantees that backup systems are reliable and operational.

The importance of strong passwords cannot be overstated. Weak passwords open doors for attackers seeking unauthorized access to sensitive files and data. Implementing strong, complex passwords that combine uppercase and lowercase letters, numbers, and symbols adds a layer of defense against brute-force attacks. Multi-factor authentication (MFA), which requires a secondary verification method beyond passwords, further enhances access control. Additionally, limiting access to sensitive files and data to authorized users or roles prevents unauthorized individuals from accessing, altering, or sharing sensitive information.

Regularly updating software and applying patches is a proactive measure that prevents attackers from exploiting known vulnerabilities. Cybercriminals often target outdated or unpatched software to infiltrate systems. Developers release updates and patches to address security vulnerabilities and improve the software's resilience against attacks. By diligently updating operating systems, applications, and security software, users mitigate the risk of falling victim to attacks that target software weaknesses.

Safe browsing practices play a crucial role in safeguarding sensitive files and data. Users should exercise caution when clicking links, downloading files, or interacting with websites requesting personal information. In order to deceive users into disclosing sensitive information, phishing attacks frequently employ misleading links and social engineering techniques. Similarly, email practices should involve verifying the sender's identity, avoiding clicking links or downloading attachments from unknown sources, and enabling spam filters to reduce the likelihood of malicious communications.

Within organizational settings, intentional and unintentional insider threats pose a significant risk to data security. Employees may inadvertently compromise sensitive information by sharing passwords or falling victim to phishing attacks. To mitigate these threats, organizations should conduct regular cybersecurity training sessions that educate employees about safe practices, recognize suspicious activities, and encourage reporting potential security incidents.

Organizations and individuals should establish data retention policies determining how long sensitive files and data are retained and when they should be securely disposed of. Retaining data beyond its useful lifespan can increase the risk of data breaches ad unauthorized access. Regularly reviewing and purging unnecessary data reduces the attack surface and minimizes the potential impact of a breach.

In the ever-evolving landscape of the digital world, safeguarding sensitive files and data is an ongoing commitment that demands vigilance, adaptability, and a collective sense of responsibility. By understanding the vulnerabilities that threaten our digital assets and implementing strategies such as encryption, secure backup, access control, and employee training, users can fortify their digital vaults against cyber threats. The responsibility transcends individual interests—it extends to organizations, communities, and society. As we navigate the intricate digital terrain, armed with knowledge and a steadfast commitment to data security, we forge a resilient digital fortress that upholds confidentiality, integrity, and the preservation of our digital legacy.

Cloud storage security and encryption

In the age of digital transformation, where data reigns supreme and accessibility is paramount, cloud storage has emerged as a revolutionary solution. It enable users to store, access, and share data seamlessly across devices and locations. However, this convenience has its challenges, as the digital realm is rife with cyber threats that can compromise the confidentiality and integrity of stored data. This section delves into the intricate landscape of cloud storage security and encryption, exploring the significance of protecting data in the cloud, the vulnerabilities that threaten cloud storage, and the strategies that empower users to navigate the ethereal realm of cloud storage with confidence and resilience.

Cloud storage epitomizes the borderless nature of the digital era, liberating data from the confines of physical storage devices. It fosters collaboration, enhances accessibility, and streamlines data management across personal, business, and organizational contexts.

However, the virtual expanse of cloud storage is accompanied by vulnerabilities that can expose data to breaches, unauthorized access, and loss. The stakes are high, as cloud storage hosts a trove of information—from personal documents and photos to proprietary business records and confidential customer data. Safeguarding this data is not just a matter of personal or organizational concern; it reflects our collective commitment to the sanctity of the digital realm.

Cloud storage, while transformative, is not immune to a range of vulnerabilities that can compromise the security of stored data. Unauthorized access, often due to weak or compromised credentials, can grant cybercriminals entry to sensitive information. Data breaches at cloud service providers can expose vast amounts of data to attackers. Whether intentional or unintentional, insider threats can lead to data leakage or unauthorized sharing. Inadequate encryption and improperly configured security settings can result in data exposure. The dynamic nature of cloud storage requires a holistic understanding of these vulnerabilities to enact comprehensive security measures.

Encryption serves as the cornerstone of cloud storage security, shielding data from unauthorized access, interception, and tampering. Encryption entails transforming data into an unreadable format using encryption algorithms. The data remains encrypted, accessible only to those with the appropriate decryption key. There are two primary forms of encryption in cloud storage: at rest and in transit. Encryption at rest guarantees that data stored on cloud servers remains encrypted even when not actively accessed. Encryption in transit safeguards data as it is transmitted between the user's device and the cloud server. Adopting strong encryption protocols is pivotal in rendering data indecipherable to attackers.

End-to-end encryption is a more robust form of data protection that extends encryption to the user's device. In this model, data is encrypted before it leaves the user's device and remains encrypted until it reaches its intended recipient. Even cloud service providers are unable to access the decrypted data. This level of encryption empowers users with greater control over their data's security and ensures that even if a breach occurs at the cloud provider's end, the data remains unintelligible to attackers.

Zero-knowledge encryption, or client-side encryption, takes data security a step further. In this approach, the cloud service provider cannot access the data, even in its encrypted form. Only the user possesses the decryption key, eliminating the risk of data exposure through provider breaches or legal demands. Zero-knowledge encryption represents the pinnacle of user-centric security, ensuring that trust in the cloud service does not come at the expense of compromising data privacy.

The security of encrypted data hinges on effective key management. The encryption key is the gateway to decrypt data, and its security is pivotal in preventing unauthorized access. Cloud service providers often offer key management services, but users must evaluate the security practices surrounding key storage and access. Storing encryption keys separate from the encrypted data adds layer of security, mitigating the risk of a single point of failure.

Multi-factor authentication (MFA) is a potent defense mechanism against unauthorized access to cloud storage accounts. It requires users to give multiple forms of verification before gaining access, usually a combination of something they know (password), something they have (a mobile device), or something they are (biometric data). MFA adds a layer of complexity for attackers seeking to breach accounts, making it significantly more challenging to compromise user credentials.

Collaboration is a hallmark of cloud storage, enabling multiple users to access and contribute to shared data. However, shared data introduces complexities in data security. Access controls, permissions, and encryption protocols must be meticulously managed to ensure that only authorized users can access, modify, or share sensitive data. Role-based access control (RBAC) can facilitate granular permissions management, ensuring that users have access only to the data necessary for their roles.

Regular auditing and monitoring of cloud storage accounts are crucial to detect unauthorized access, unusual activities, or potential breaches. Cloud service providers often offer logging and monitoring features that enable users to track user activity, access history, and security events. Consistently reviewing these logs and responding to suspicious activities can help detect and thwart potential threats in real time.

Cloud storage represents a paradigm shift in storing and interacting with data—a celestial realm where convenience converges with complexity. Safeguarding sensitive data in this realm is a responsibility that demands unwavering commitment and a multi-faceted approach. By understanding the vulnerabilities inherent in cloud storage, embracing encryption and security protocols, and adopting practices such as end-to-end encryption and zero-knowledge encryption, users can navigate the ethereal realm with security and confidence. The journey transcends personal and organizational interests; it is a shared endeavor that upholds the sanctity of data, fortifies trust, and ensures that the celestial expanse of cloud storage remains a bastion of security—a reflection of our collective dedication to preserving the integrity of the digital realm.

Importance of regular backups

In the intricate tapestry of the digital age, where our lives and businesses are interwoven with technology, the importance of regular backups emerges as a cornerstone of digital resilience. Our digital footprints span across personal memories, sensitive documents, critical business data, and irreplaceable information. However, the digital landscape is not impervious to risks—from hardware failures and cyber threats to accidental deletions and natural disasters—that can abruptly sever our access to these digital assets. This section delves into the multifaceted significance of regular backups, exploring the vulnerabilities that underscore the need for backups, the types of backup strategies available, and the strategies that empower individuals and organizations to cultivate a culture of digital preparedness.

In the digital realm, vulnerabilities abound, casting a shadow over the sanctity of our data and information. Hardware failures, including malfunctioning hard drives and storage devices, can permanently lose data. Cyber threats, such as ransomware attacks and malware infections, can encrypt or corrupt data, rendering it inaccessible until a ransom is paid or the infection is mitigated. Accidental deletions, often triggered by human error, can erase precious memories, documents, and records. Natural disasters, ranging from fires to floods, can obliterate physical devices housing our digital assets. These vulnerabilities underscore the fragility of our digital existence and emphasize the imperative of adopting strategies that ensure data survivability.

Regular backups are a digital safety net that safeguards against data loss and disruption. A backup entails creating copies of data and storing them in secure locations—external hard drives, cloud storage, or dedicated backup servers. The essence of backups lies in redundancy: having multiple copies of data ensures that if one copy is compromised or inaccessible, another remains intact. Backups enable data recovery in the face of hardware failures, cyber attacks, accidental deletions, and other unforeseen events that threaten the integrity of digital assets.

The realm of backups encompasses a spectrum of strategies that cater to diverse needs and levels of data criticality. Full backups involve copying all data to a backup location, offering comprehensive protection but requiring substantial storage space and time. Incremental backups capture only changes made since the last backup, conserving storage space and expediting the backup process. Differential backups strike a balance by capturing changes since the previous full backup, simplifying the restoration process while consuming less space than full backups. Continuous or real-time backups automatically synchronize data changes with the backup location as they occur, offering near-instantaneous data protection. The choice of backup strategy depends on data volume, criticality, available resources, and recovery time objectives.

The efficacy of backups extends beyond data recovery—it permeates the realm of business continuity. Data is the lifeblood for organizations that fuel operations, decision-making, and customer interactions. The ability to swiftly recover from data disruptions directly impacts business resilience. Backups ensure that in the event of data loss, data corruption, or cyber attacks, organizations can restore critical systems and processes with minimal downtime. This rapid restoration translates into minimized business disruption, reduced financial losses, and the preservation of customer trust.

Remote and offsite backups add an extra layer of protection against localized disasters. Storing backups in a geographically distant location reduces the risk of simultaneous loss due to a localized event, such as a fire or flood. Cloud storage, a popular choice for remote backups, offers the advantage of scalability, accessibility, and automated backups. Cloud providers typically implement redundant storage and security measures that fortify data against loss and unauthorized access.

Automated backups streamline the backup process and bolster reliability. Manually initiating backups can be prone to oversight and negligence. On the other hand, automated backup solutions ensure that backups are executed at predefined intervals without requiring user intervention. This approach reduces the danger of data loss due to forgetfulness or human error, enhancing the consistency and effectiveness of the backup strategy.

An often-overlooked aspect of backups is data retention and versioning. Backing up data at regular intervals creates a timeline of data versions, preserving historical context and enabling the recovery of specific versions of files. This feature proves invaluable when restoring a file to a state before it was corrupted or modified in error. Versioning empowers users and organizations to navigate the temporal landscape of their digital assets, enhancing data recovery precision.

Embracing the practice of regular backups requires a shift in mindset—an acknowledgment of the impermanence of digital assets and the proactive measures needed to counteract it. Individuals and organizations must cultivate a culture of digital preparedness that integrates backups into daily routines and operational strategies. This entails setting backup schedules, periodically verifying the integrity of backup copies, and adapting backup strategies as data volumes and criticality evolve.

In the grand tapestry of the digital era, regular backups emerge as the threads that weave resilience into the fabric of our digital existence. They act as sentinels against the vulnerabilities that cast shadows over our data, offering a lifeline in the face of data loss, cyber attacks, and unforeseen events. By understanding the vulnerabilities that threaten our digital assets, adopting a suitable backup strategy, and fostering a culture of digital preparedness, individuals and organizations empower themselves with the tools needed to navigate the digital landscape with confidence. The journey transcends the realm of technology—it reflects a commitment to preserving the digital legacies we create, safeguarding memories, enabling business continuity, and upholding the sanctity of our digital identity. As we traverse the dynamic terrain of the digital age, let us embrace the importance of regular backups as a beacon of digital resilience—a testament to our determination to protect what matters most in the ethereal realm of data.

CHAPTER VIII

Social Engineering and Human Factors

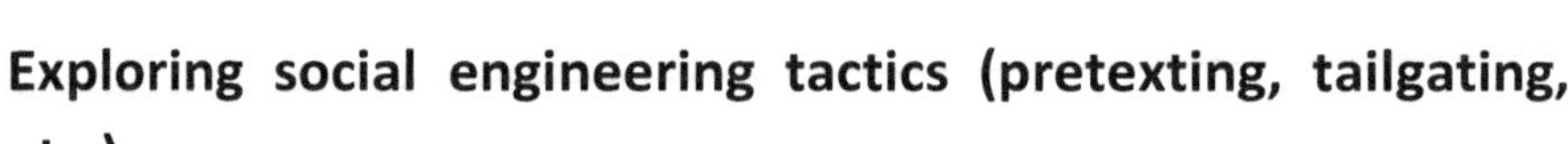

Exploring social engineering tactics (pretexting, tailgating, etc.)

In the complex interplay of the digital age, where technology intertwines with human psychology, social engineering tactics have emerged as formidable weapons in the hands of cybercriminals. These tactics exploit human vulnerabilities, leveraging trust, empathy, and curiosity to manipulate individuals into divulging sensitive information, granting unauthorized access, or performing actions compromising security. This section delves into the intricate world of social engineering tactics, exploring the psychology behind these techniques, the types of tactics employed—such as pretexting and tailgating—and strategies to defend against these insidious forms of deception.

Social engineering tactics are rooted in the fundamental understanding of human behavior and cognitive biases. Cybercriminals recognize that technology alone may be impenetrable, but the human element—the propensity to trust, the desire to help, and the inclination to comply with authority—can be exploited to breach digital defenses. Social engineers use emotions, fears, and desires to manipulate targets, making them unwitting accomplices in their own security breaches.

Pretexting is a masterclass in storytelling. It involves creating a fabricated scenario to manipulate individuals into revealing sensitive information. The social engineer assumes a fictitious identity—a coworker, a bank representative, a tech support agent—and weaves a convincing narrative to evoke trust and credibility. Victims are prompted to provide personal or confidential information to address a legitimate concern. Pretexting exploits empathy and trust to breach security barriers, whether posing as a colleague needing assistance or a service provider requiring verification.

In the realm of cybersecurity, not all threats originate from behind screens. Tailgating capitalizes on the physical vulnerabilities of access control systems. The premise is simple: the social engineer gains unauthorized entry into a secured facility by closely following an authorized individual through controlled access points. The technique exploits the natural tendency to hold the door for others and bypasses security measures that are predicated on the assumption that only authorized personnel will enter.

Quid pro quo capitalizes on the principle of reciprocity. The social engineer offers something of perceived value—a service, a software upgrade, or assistance—in exchange for sensitive information. This tactic exploits the psychological desire to reciprocate favors and create a sense of indebtedness. Victims may readily provide information, such as passwords or access credentials, in exchange for the promised benefit, inadvertently granting the social engineer access to their digital assets.

Phishing is perhaps the most recognizable social engineering tactic, proliferating through emails, text messages, and instant messaging platforms. The attacker impersonates a legitimate entity—such as a bank, a social media platform, or a reputable organization—and lures victims into clicking on malicious links or downloading infected attachments. Phishing exploits urgency, curiosity, and fear to prompt victims into taking actions that compromise their security, such as revealing login credentials or installing malware.

Baiting tantalizes victims with offers too enticing to resist. Cybercriminals distribute malicious content—often disguised as free software, music, movies, or physical items—through unofficial channels. The allure of something for nothing leads victims to download or install the bait, unknowingly infecting their devices with malware or granting unauthorized access. Baiting leverages human curiosity and the desire for immediate gratification to breach digital defenses.

Defending against social engineering tactics requires a multifaceted approach that blends awareness, education, and technological safeguards.

Education is a cornerstone of defense. Individuals who receive regular security awareness training are better equipped to spot and counteract social engineering techniques. Training programs foster skepticism and critical thinking and empower individuals to question unusual requests, verify identities, and discern between legitimate and malicious communications.

Verifying the legitimacy of requests is paramount. When faced with a request for sensitive information or actions that deviate from routine, individuals should independently confirm the requester's identity through established communication channels. For instance, contacting the supposed sender of an email through a known phone number—rather than replying directly—can mitigate the risk of falling victim to impersonation.

Multi-factor authentication (MFA) is a robust defense mechanism that thwarts many social engineering tactics. Even if attackers manage to gather login credentials, MFA requires an additional form of verification—such as a temporary code sent to a trusted device—to access an account. This layer of protection significantly reduces the risk of unauthorized access.

Organizations should establish and enforce security policies and procedures that govern data sharing, access controls, and communication protocols. Clear guidelines regarding sharing sensitive information and the processes for verifying requests can fortify defenses against social engineering tactics.

Instilling a healthy dose of skepticism is a potent defense mechanism. Encouraging individuals to question unusual requests, assess the legitimacy of offers, and scrutinize the veracity of stories can create a psychological barrier against social engineering tactics.

The realm of social engineering tactics is a testament to the convergence of human psychology and technological exploitation. Cybercriminals harness emotions, trust, and cognitive biases to breach digital defenses. Individuals and organizations can fortify their digital resilience by understanding the psychology behind these tactics—such as pretexting, tailgating, and quid pro quo. Vigilance, education, and the cultivation of a skeptical mindset empower us to navigate the intricate art of deception with caution, emerging unscathed in the dynamic landscape of the digital age.

Enhancing awareness of manipulation techniques

In the intricate realm of the digital age, where information flows ceaselessly and connections span the globe, the awareness of manipulation techniques has emerged as a crucial defense mechanism against the insidious tactics employed by malicious actors. Manipulation techniques leverage psychological triggers, cognitive biases, and emotional vulnerabilities to sway decisions, extract sensitive information, or compromise digital security. This section delves into the profound significance of enhancing awareness of manipulation techniques, exploring the psychology behind these tactics, common manipulation methods, and strategies to empower individuals to fortify their defenses against manipulation in online and offline interactions.

At the heart of manipulation techniques lies a profound understanding of human psychology. Malicious actors recognize that individuals are susceptible to cognitive biases, emotional triggers, and social pressures that can influence their behavior and decisions.

By tapping into these vulnerabilities, manipulators aim to control perceptions, shape opinions, and achieve their objectives—whether that involves obtaining sensitive information, swaying political views, or engaging in fraudulent activities.

Manipulation techniques encompass a diverse array of tactics that exploit psychological vulnerabilities. Gaslighting involves distorting reality to make victims doubt their perceptions or sanity, creating a sense of confusion and dependency. Emotional manipulation leverages guilt, fear, or affection to control behavior or extract concessions. Misinformation and disinformation spread false or misleading information to shape opinions or undermine trust in reliable sources. Cults and extremist groups employ brainwashing techniques to isolate individuals, control their thoughts, and foster loyalty to the group. In the digital realm, clickbait headlines and sensationalized content exploit curiosity and emotional triggers to attract clicks and engagement.

Enhancing awareness of manipulation techniques begins with cultivating critical thinking skills. Individuals must question information sources, evaluate the credibility of claims, and consider the motivations behind messages. Fact-checking and cross-referencing information with reputable sources can help unveil inaccuracies and falsehoods. By approaching information with skepticism and a discerning mindset, individuals can mitigate the risk of falling victim to manipulation.

Cognitive biases are organized patterns of rationality deviation that frequently result in inaccurate conclusions. Anchoring bias involves fixating on the first piece of information encountered, influencing subsequent decisions. Confirmation bias drives individuals to seek and interpret information that aligns with preexisting beliefs, reinforcing echo chambers. Availability bias prioritizes easily accessible information over comprehensive data, potentially leading to skewed perceptions. By recognizing these biases, individuals can consciously counteract their effects, seeking diverse perspectives and carefully assessing information.

Media literacy is a vital skill in an era characterized by information overload. Media literacy empowers individuals to critically analyze and interpret media messages, discerning between reliable journalism and sensationalism. By learning to identify bias, verify sources, and distinguish between news and opinion, individuals can discern the information landscape and make informed decisions.

Awareness of manipulation techniques is essential in online interactions for safeguarding digital dialogues. Phishing emails prey on urgency, curiosity, or fear to prompt recipients to click on malicious links or divulge sensitive information. Social engineering tactics exploit trust, empathy, and authority to manipulate individuals into revealing passwords, personal details, or access credentials. Being cautious of unsolicited requests, verifying the identity of senders, and refraining from sharing personal or sensitive information can mitigate the risk of falling victim to online manipulation.

Emotional manipulation often targets vulnerabilities such as empathy, guilt, and fear. Building emotional resilience involves recognizing and managing these emotions. By setting healthy boundaries, engaging in open communication, and seeking support from trusted individuals, individuals can shield themselves from emotional exploitation and manipulation.

Education and training initiatives are pivotal in enhancing awareness of manipulation techniques. Organizations, schools, and communities can offer workshops, seminars, and resources that equip individuals with the tools to recognize and resist manipulation. By fostering a culture of critical thinking, open discourse, and skepticism, these initiatives empower individuals to navigate the complexities of the digital age with resilience and vigilance.

The imperative of enhancing awareness of manipulation techniques reflects the evolving nature of the digital landscape—a realm where information, opinions, and intentions intermingle in intricate ways. By understanding the psychology behind manipulation, recognizing common tactics, and cultivating critical thinking skills, individuals and communities can fortify their defenses against manipulation's insidious grasp. The journey transcends the confines of screens and extends to our interactions, decisions, and perceptions—transforming awareness into a shield that safeguards against deception, preserves autonomy, and upholds the principles of digital resilience in an age defined by complexity and connection.

Training employees and family members to recognize and respond to social engineering attempts

In the intricate tapestry of the digital age, where connectivity and communication bridge vast distances, the role of training employees and family members to recognize and respond to social engineering attempts emerges as a linchpin of digital security. Social engineering tactics exploit human vulnerabilities, leveraging trust, curiosity, and authority to manipulate individuals into divulging sensitive information or compromising their safety. This section delves into the vital importance of training in the context of social engineering, exploring the significance of training both employees within organizations and family members in domestic settings. It examines the rationale behind such training, the methods employed to impart awareness and resilience, and the strategies that empower individuals to stand resilient against the myriad forms of digital manipulation.

In cybersecurity, the weakest link often lies not in the technology itself, but in the human element. Malicious actors capitalize on psychological vulnerabilities to bypass digital defenses. This highlights the criticality of arming both employees and family members with the knowledge and tools to recognize and respond to social engineering attempts. Training is a proactive measure to mitigate the risks posed by manipulation tactics, ensuring that individuals are equipped to make informed decisions, assess the legitimacy of requests, and safeguard their digital and personal assets.

Organizations are prime targets for social engineering attacks, given the potential for massive data breaches, financial losses, and reputational damage. Training employees to be vigilant against manipulation techniques is pivotal in bolstering the organization's overall cybersecurity posture. It cultivates a culture of digital resilience where employees recognize the value of their actions in protecting sensitive data and critical systems. Through workshops, simulations, and case studies, employees can learn to identify phishing emails, resist emotional manipulation, verify the authenticity of requests, and report suspicious activities. This proactive approach fortifies the organization's defenses and fosters a sense of collective responsibility toward cybersecurity.

Training programs employ various methods to instill awareness and resilience in the face of social engineering attempts. Simulated phishing exercises expose employees to realistic phishing scenarios, enabling them to experience the tactics firsthand and learn to discern between legitimate and malicious communications. Role-playing scenarios allow participants to practice responding to social engineering tactics, enhancing their confidence and decision-making abilities. Case studies of real-world social engineering incidents provide insights into the tactics used, the consequences of falling victim, and the strategies that could have prevented the attack.

Key to training individuals to recognize and respond to social engineering attempts is helping them identify manipulation tactics. Participants learn to recognize red flags—such as urgent requests for sensitive information, unsolicited emails from unknown senders, and recommendations for password resets—and develop the skepticism needed to question unusual requests. They are encouraged to independently verify the requester's identity through established communication channels, even if the request comes from a legitimate source.

Effective training goes beyond recognition—it equips individuals with response strategies that minimize the impact of social engineering attempts. Participants learn to report suspicious activities to designated security personnel, enabling prompt action and incident mitigation. Additionally, training emphasizes the importance of emotional resilience, helping individuals withstand emotional manipulation tactics by setting healthy boundaries, seeking support, and practicing self-awareness.

While organizational training strengthens the frontline against cyber threats, training family members is equally essential in safeguarding the homefront. Individuals' digital lives extend beyond the workplace, encompassing personal communications, financial transactions, and sensitive data shared within the family circle. By training family members to recognize manipulation tactics, households can collectively fortify their digital resilience. Family members learn to identify potential scams targeting seniors, children, and adolescents, and develop strategies to protect personal information and respond to suspicious requests.

Training employees and family members to recognize and respond to social engineering attempts fosters a culture of vigilance that transcends individual actions. Within organizations, this culture permeates daily operations, enhancing cybersecurity practices, reducing the risk of successful attacks, and instilling a sense of collective responsibility. It bolsters trust and open communication in family settings, enabling family members to defend against manipulation attempts collectively.

In the realm where human psychology and technology intersect, training employees and family members to recognize and respond to social engineering attempts become a beacon of digital empowerment. By imparting knowledge, cultivating awareness, and fostering the ability to discern manipulation tactics, individuals stand resilient against the deceptive forces that seek to exploit their vulnerabilities. The journey transcends the confines of offices and homes, touching the fabric of the digital age itself—an age defined by connectivity, complexity, and the shared responsibility to safeguard the sanctity of the digital realm. Through training, we illuminate the path toward digital empowerment—a way that empowers us to navigate the intricate landscape of manipulation with vigilance, confidence, and the unwavering determination to protect what matters most.

CHAPTER IX

Business and
Corporate Cybersecurity

Cybersecurity challenges in a business environment

In the dynamic landscape of modern business, where technology drives operations and connectivity fuels growth, cybersecurity challenges have emerged as a critical consideration for enterprises of all sizes. Organizations must contend with a variety of cyber threats as they embrace digital transformation and the advantages of networked systems. These threats can compromise sensitive data, cause disruptions in business operations, and erode public trust. This section delves into the multifaceted cybersecurity challenges that businesses encounter in their environment, examining the evolving threat landscape, the vulnerabilities specific to business operations, and the strategies that empower organizations to fortify their digital defenses.

The digital era has ushered in a new age of cyber threats, marked by their sophistication, diversity, and global reach. Malicious actors exploit software, networks, and human behavior vulnerabilities to gain unauthorized access, launch attacks, and steal valuable data.

From the rapid rise of ransomware attacks that encrypt critical systems and demand hefty ransoms for decryption keys, to sophisticated phishing campaigns that trick employees into revealing sensitive information, the threat landscape is marked by its complexity and adaptability.

Businesses operate within an intricate ecosystem of networks, devices, applications, and personnel, all of which can introduce vulnerabilities if not properly secured. Insider threats from employees or contractors can result in data breaches or the unintentional exposure of sensitive information. Bring Your Own Device (also known as BYOD) policies are increasingly common, which increases the risk of unwanted access and data leakage. Third-party vendors and suppliers, often granted access to internal systems, introduce additional points of exposure that cybercriminals can exploit.

As governments around the world enact stringent data protection and privacy regulations, businesses are grappling with compliance challenges. Regulations such as the General Data Protection Regulation (also known as GDPR) and the California Consumer Privacy Act (also known as CCPA) impose strict data handling, consent, and breach reporting requirements. Non-compliance leads to potential legal repercussions, erodes consumer trust, and damages reputation. Balancing compliance demands with effective cybersecurity measures is a delicate tightrope that businesses must navigate.

The most potent vulnerabilities often lie in the human element. Phishing attacks and social engineering techniques take advantage of psychological tricks to get people to reveal sensitive information or take security-compromising activities. Business employees, ranging from entry-level staff to top executives, are targets for cybercriminals seeking unauthorized access to systems, financial information, and proprietary data. Even with sophisticated technological safeguards in place, a single employee falling victim to a well-crafted phishing email can open the door to a significant breach.

A workforce that lacks security awareness poses a substantial risk. Employees unaware of cybersecurity best practices may inadvertently compromise data by clicking on malicious links, downloading infected attachments, or sharing sensitive information. Comprehensive security awareness training programs are crucial in bridging the knowledge gap and empowering employees to recognize and respond to cyber threats. Education equips them with the skills to identify phishing attempts, report suspicious activities, and make informed decisions that bolster the organization's security posture.

Cybercriminals are adept at adapting their tactics to exploit new attack vectors. As organizations adopt cloud computing, the Internet of Things (IoT), and other emerging technologies, new avenues for cyber attacks emerge. Attacks targeting cloud environments can lead to data breaches and compromise sensitive information. Insecure IoT devices can be exploited to gain unauthorized access to networks or launch distributed denial-of-service (DDoS) attacks. The rapidly evolving nature of technology demands a cybersecurity strategy that remains adaptable and responsive.

Resource constraints are a challenge many organizations face when it comes to cybersecurity. The costs associated with implementing robust security measures—such as investing in advanced cybersecurity solutions, hiring skilled professionals, and conducting regular security assessments—can strain budgets. As a result, businesses can be forced to make challenging decisions regarding how to distribute their resources. Striking a balance between cost-effective solutions and comprehensive protection is a delicate exercise that requires careful consideration.

In modern business, cybersecurity challenges loom large, testing the resilience and agility of organizations as they navigate the digital battleground. The evolving threat landscape, human vulnerabilities, regulatory demands, and resource constraints all contribute to the complexity of the cybersecurity landscape. However, the challenges are not insurmountable. By embracing a proactive approach, prioritizing security awareness training, fostering a culture of cybersecurity vigilance, and adopting comprehensive defense strategies, businesses can stand resilient against the multifaceted threats that seek to compromise their operations, data, and reputation. The journey transcends technology—it reflects a commitment to safeguarding digital assets and the trust of customers, partners, and stakeholders who rely on the organization's commitment to security in an age where the digital realm and the business environment are increasingly intertwined.

Protecting customer data and sensitive business information

In the interconnected landscape of modern business, where data flows seamlessly and digital transactions underpin every operation, customer data and sensitive business information protection have risen to paramount importance. As organizations embrace the benefits of technology-driven operations and digital customer interactions, securing this data against cyber threats and breaches becomes a cornerstone of ethical business practices. This section delves into the imperative of safeguarding customer data and sensitive business information, exploring the ethical obligations, the risks posed by data breaches, and the strategies that empower businesses to uphold the trust placed in them by customers and partners.

Organizations function as custodians of the data entrusted to them by customers, clients, and partners. This custodianship carries with it an ethical imperative to protect this data's privacy, confidentiality, and integrity. When customers share their personal information or engage in transactions, they expect their data to be handled responsibly and securely. Organizations must honor this trust by implementing robust cybersecurity measures that prevent unauthorized access, data breaches, and the misuse of sensitive information.

The consequences of data breaches extend far beyond the confines of technology. A single breach can have cascading effects, resulting in financial losses, reputational damage, legal repercussions, and erosion of customer trust. Financial losses can arise from the costs of remediating the breach, compensating affected parties, and addressing regulatory fines. Reputational damage can tarnish an organization's brand, eroding the hard-earned trust of customers and stakeholders. Legal repercussions stem from violations of data protection regulations, leading to legal battles and further financial strain. Ultimately, the fallout from a data breach can lead to losing customer loyalty and business opportunities.

Compliance is not only an option but a legal requirement in an era distinguished by strict data protection laws which include the Health Insurance Portability and Accountability Act (or simply HIPAA) and the General Data Protection Regulation (also known as GDPR). Organizations that fail to implement appropriate security measures or mishandle customer data can face significant fines, lawsuits, and reputational damage. Compliance with these regulations necessitates a comprehensive understanding of data handling practices, consent requirements, breach notification obligations, and data subject rights. Organizations are committed to accountability and transparency by aligning their practices with these regulations.

Protecting customer data and sensitive business information requires a cultural shift that permeates every level of the organization. Leadership must champion cybersecurity as a core value, prioritizing it in strategic decisions and resource allocation. However, cybersecurity is not solely the responsibility of IT departments—it is a collective effort that involves every employee, from executives to frontline staff. Comprehensive security awareness training programs empower employees to recognize phishing attempts, report suspicious activities, and adhere to best practices. A culture of cybersecurity awareness and vigilance serves as a potent defense against the multitude of threats that target sensitive data.

Technological safeguards form the backbone of data protection strategies. Encryption of data both in transit and at rest ensures that even if unauthorized access occurs, the data remains incomprehensible without the appropriate decryption keys. Multi-factor authentication (MFA) adds a futher layer of defense, requiring users to provide multiple verification forms to access sensitive information. Regular software updates and security patches mitigate vulnerabilities that cybercriminals can exploit. Intrusion detection systems and firewalls serve as sentinels, monitoring network traffic and filtering out potentially malicious activities.

Businesses often collaborate with third-party vendors and partners, sharing data and accessing each other's systems. However, this collaboration introduces additional points of vulnerability. Organizations must ensure that vendors adhere to robust cybersecurity practices and data protection standards. Contracts and agreements should include clauses outlining data protection responsibilities and breach notification protocols. By extending the cybersecurity perimeter to include partners and vendors, organizations create a more fortified defense against data breaches that could originate from external sources.

While prevention is crucial, organizations must also prepare for the eventuality of a data breach. Incident response planning involves developing a comprehensive strategy that outlines the steps to take in case of a breach. This includes identifying a dedicated incident response team, defining communication protocols, notifying affected parties, and remediating the breach. A well-prepared incident response plan minimizes the impact of a breach, enhances the organization's ability to recover, and showcases the commitment to responsible data handling.

In a digital landscape where data is both an asset and a liability, organizations assume the role of guardians of digital trust. By protecting customer data and sensitive business information, they demonstrate their commitment to ethical practices, regulatory compliance, and the preservation of customer confidence. The responsibility transcends technology and reflects the values, ethics, and integrity underpinning every interaction and transaction. As organizations navigate the complexities of the digital age, they must recognize that data protection is not a mere obligation—it is a testament to their dedication to the security, privacy, and trust of the individuals and entities that rely on their digital custodianship.

Creating a cybersecurity policy and incident response plan

In the rapidly evolving landscape of digital connectivity, where technology intertwines with every facet of modern operations, creating a robust cybersecurity policy and incident response plan has become paramount for organizations seeking to navigate the complex realm of cyber threats. As cyberattacks become increasingly sophisticated and prevalent, organizations must proactively fortify their defenses by establishing comprehensive frameworks that outline security practices, protocols, and strategies for effectively responding to breaches. This section delves into the imperative of crafting a cybersecurity policy and incident response plan, exploring their roles in bolstering digital resilience, the key components of each, and how they synergistically safeguard the integrity of operations and the trust of stakeholders.

A cybersecurity policy is a blueprint that guides an organization's approach to safeguarding its digital assets, sensitive data, and overall security posture. It articulates the organization's commitment to security, establishes technology usage guidelines, and outlines employees' responsibilities in upholding these practices. From password management and access controls to data encryption and remote work security, a well-crafted cybersecurity policy encompasses various measures that collectively contribute to creating a robust digital defense.

An effective cybersecurity policy comprises several vital components that lay the foundation for a proactive security approach. A clear statement of purpose communicates the organization's commitment to protecting its digital infrastructure and the sensitive information it holds. Access control and authentication protocols detail how access to systems and data is managed and secured, preventing unauthorized access. Data handling procedures define how sensitive information is stored, transmitted, and disposed of, ensuring compliance with relevant regulations. Incident reporting procedures facilitate the timely reporting and resolution of security incidents, promoting transparency and swift action.

The strategic framework known as an incident response plan describes the actions that a company will take in case of a cybersecurity breach or incident. Organizations may lessen the impact of a breach, cut downtime, and ensure a well-coordinated and effective response by adopting a well-defined strategy in preparation. An incident response plan bridges the gap between the occurrence of a breach and the restoration of normalcy, mitigating the potential for further damage and providing a clear roadmap for restoring operations.

An effective incident response plan comprises a series of well-defined stages that address every facet of a cybersecurity incident. Detection and identification involve recognizing and confirming the occurrence of a breach. Containment entails isolating the affected systems and preventing the breach from spreading. Eradication focuses on removing the root cause of the breach, ensuring that the organization's systems are no longer vulnerable. Recovery involves restoring affected systems and data to their pre-incident state. Post-incident analysis and lessons learned to ensure that the organization gains insights from the breach, strengthens its defenses, and continually improves its incident response capabilities.

Creating a cybersecurity policy and incident response plan is not a dualistic endeavor—it represents a symbiotic relationship that comprehensively fortifies an organization's security posture. A robust cybersecurity policy establishes a proactive foundation by outlining preventive measures, security practices, and the responsibilities of individuals across the organization. On the other hand, an incident response plan prepares for the inevitable by providing a structured approach to handling breaches, minimizing their impact, and expediting recovery. Together, these two frameworks create a holistic defense strategy that addresses prevention, detection, response, and recovery—enabling organizations to navigate the digital landscape with resilience and confidence.

The efficacy of a cybersecurity policy and incident response plan hinges on their integration into the organization's culture. Training programs and awareness initiatives empower employees at all levels to understand their role in cybersecurity, recognize potential threats, and respond effectively. A security culture emphasizes individual responsibility, promotes transparency in reporting incidents, and fosters an environment where continuous improvement is valued. When stakeholders are actively engaged in the execution of these frameworks, the organization's digital resilience is fortified from within.

Cybersecurity is not static—it requires ongoing evaluation, adaptation, and refinement. Organizations must reassess their cybersecurity policies and incident response plans as the threat landscape evolves to ensure they remain effective. Regular penetration testing, vulnerability assessments, as well as scenario-based exercises can show where improvements need to be made and how new best practices can be added. A dynamic approach to cybersecurity ensures that policies and plans remain relevant and resilient in the face of ever-evolving cyber threats.

Creating a cybersecurity policy and incident response plan is indispensable in an era of digital innovation and interconnectedness. These frameworks are not mere documents—they are the instruments that empower organizations to navigate the complexities of the digital age with confidence, resilience, and a steadfast commitment to protecting their operations, data, and stakeholders. By forging a path of proactive prevention, rapid response, and continuous improvement, organizations can transcend the vulnerabilities of the digital landscape, fortifying their digital resilience and embodying a culture that places security at the forefront of their endeavors.

CHAPTER X

Emerging Threats and Future Trends

Overview of new and evolving cyber threats

In the dynamic and interconnected realm of the digital age, where innovation and connectivity drive progress, the landscape of cyber threats is undergoing a rapid and continuous evolution. The methods used by malicious actors looking to exploit vulnerabilities, compromise data, and interfere with operations also progress along with technology. This section provides an overview of the new and evolving cyber threats that organizations and individuals face, highlighting the emergence of novel attack vectors, the sophistication of techniques, and the imperative of staying vigilant in an ever-changing digital landscape.

Ransomware, a type of malware that encrypts an organization's data until a ransom is paid, has taken on new dimensions. While traditional ransomware focused solely on encryption, attackers now employ a tactic known as "double extortion." In this scenario, the victim's data is encrypted, and a copy is also exfiltrated before encryption. Threat actors threaten to release the stolen data publicly if the ransom is not paid. This evolution increases the pressure on organizations to comply with ransom demands and highlights the importance of robust backup and recovery strategies as a defense against extortion.

Supply chain attacks have gained prominence as cybercriminals recognize the potential impact of compromising trusted software providers or vendors. By infiltrating a trusted supply chain partner, attackers can deliver malware to a broader range of targets that rely on the compromised software. The SolarWinds incident of 2020 is a notable example where malicious actors inserted malware into legitimate software updates, impacting numerous organizations. The complexity of modern supply chains demands increased diligence in vendor assessment and security measures.

Zero-day exploits target vulnerabilities that are unknown to software vendors and therefore, unpatched. These vulnerabilities are exploited by attackers to breach systems, gain unauthorized access, and steal data. The increasing value of zero-day exploits in the cybercriminal ecosystem has led to a thriving market for their discovery and sale. Organizations must rely on proactive security measures beyond patching, such as intrusion detection systems and behavior-based analytics, to identify and mitigate threats leveraging these vulnerabilities.

While artificial intelligence (AI) and machine learning (ML) have brought innovation to cybersecurity, they have also introduced new threats. Malicious actors can leverage AI and ML to automate attacks, tailor phishing emails, or even evade detection by security systems. Conversely, cybersecurity professionals also deploy AI and

ML to identify behavior patterns indicative of attacks. The ongoing interplay between AI-driven attacks and AI-enhanced defenses showcases the rapid evolution of the cyber threat landscape.

As the Internet of Things expands, so does the attack surface for cyber threats. IoT devices, often designed with convenience in mind, may lack robust security measures, making them attractive targets for attackers. Botnets composed of compromised IoT devices can be used to launch large-scale distributed denial-of-service (DDoS) attacks. Organizations and individuals must prioritize securing IoT devices through proper configuration, regular updates, and network segmentation.

Phishing attacks have evolved beyond generic emails with spelling errors. Attackers now employ sophisticated tactics known as "spear phishing" and "whaling," which involve personalized and compelling messages targeting specific individuals or high-value targets. These emails often mimic trusted contacts' tone and language, making them difficult to discern from genuine communication. Robust employee training, multi-factor authentication, and email verification protocols are crucial defenses against these refined phishing tactics.

Social engineering remains a potent tool for cybercriminals, who exploit human psychology to manipulate individuals into either divulging sensitive information or performing actions that compromise security. While traditional social engineering tactics like pretexting and baiting persist, attackers also leverage emotional manipulation, exploit current events, and use deepfake technology to manipulate video and audio content. Educating individuals about the psychology of manipulation and fostering a culture of skepticism are essential defenses against these evolving tactics.

The overview of new and evolving cyber threats underscores the dynamic and ever-changing nature of the digital battlefield. The landscape is marked by continuous innovation—the attackers refining their techniques and organizations strengthening their defenses. Staying ahead requires a multi-faceted approach: proactive cybersecurity measures, robust incident response plans, continuous security training, and a commitment to adaptability. Collaboration between individuals, organizations, and security professionals is paramount in this landscape. As the digital realm continues to shape our lives and society, the vigilance and preparedness to counter emerging cyber threats will determine the resilience of our digital future.

The role of artificial intelligence as well as machine learning in cybersecurity

In the era of rapid digital transformation, where technology permeates every facet of modern life, the role of artificial intelligence (AI) as well as machine learning (ML) in cybersecurity has emerged as a transformative force. Traditional cybersecurity procedures are unable to keep up with the evolution of cyber threats, which are becoming more complex and dynamic. A paradigm change is provided by AI and ML, which give enterprises the capabilities they need to proactively identify, address, and mitigate cyberthreats in real time. This section delves into the multifaceted role of AI and ML in cybersecurity, exploring their application across prevention, detection, response, and prediction, and highlighting their potential in shaping the future of digital defense.

One of the most prominent applications of AI and ML in cybersecurity is threat detection. Traditional signature-based approaches to detection often fall short against emerging and novel threats. AI and ML algorithms, however, excel in identifying anomalies in vast datasets, thereby identifying previously unseen patterns that might indicate a cyber attack. Machine-learning algorithms can be trained using historical data to identify typical behavior, allowing them to flag deviations that might be a sign of malicious activity. Organizations are able to recognize threats and take action before they worsen due to this ability to spot subtle deviations in real-time.

Human behavior lies at the heart of many cyber threats, and AI and ML have proven invaluable in understanding and predicting these behaviors. Behavioral analytics leverage machine learning to analyze patterns in user behavior, allowing organizations to identify deviations from ordinary activities. For instance, if an employee suddenly accesses sensitive data at an unusual time or from a unique location, behavioral analytics can trigger alerts, enabling organizations to investigate potential insider threats or compromised accounts. By understanding human behavior, AI and ML enhance organizations' ability to thwart attacks that exploit human vulnerabilities.

Incident response is a critical component of cybersecurity, and AI and ML can significantly expedite this process. These technologies can identify the attack's origin and its effects by analyzing massive amounts of data produced during a breach. This real-time analysis lets security teams make informed decisions quickly, minimizing downtime and potential damage. Furthermore, AI can automate specific incident response tasks, such as isolating affected systems or quarantining compromised accounts, allowing human analysts to focus on strategic decision-making and comprehensive threat mitigation.

The ability of AI and ML to analyze historical data and identify patterns extends to predicting future threats. Machine learning models can predict potential attack vectors and vulnerabilities by analyzing past cyber attack data. This proactive approach allows organizations to prioritize patching, fortify defenses, and allocate resources effectively. Predictive analysis shifts cybersecurity from a reactive stance to a proactive one, where organizations anticipate and neutralize threats before they materialize.

Threat hunting involves proactively seeking out signs of cyber threats that may have evaded automated detection. By sifting through enormous amounts of data to find minor signs of compromise, AI and ML can improve this process. These technologies can unearth hidden threats that may have bypassed traditional defenses by analyzing network traffic, log data, and other digital footprints. Threat hunters with AI-powered tools are better equipped to identify and neutralize threats lurking in an organization's digital landscape.

While integrating AI and ML in cybersecurity offers immense potential, it also comes with challenges and ethical considerations. The effectiveness of machine learning models relies heavily on the data quality used for training. Biased or incomplete datasets can lead to skewed results, potentially amplifying existing inequalities or missing specific threat indicators. Additionally, the increasing automation of cybersecurity tasks raises questions about the potential for false positives or negatives and the implications of relying solely on algorithms for decision-making. Balancing innovation and responsible use of AI and ML requires transparency, ongoing monitoring, and a commitment to addressing potential biases.

Artificial intelligence and machine learning's impact on cybersecurity is not a fleeting trend; rather, it is a revolutionary force that will change the face of digital defense. AI and ML algorithms are poised to become the cornerstone of adaptive cyber defense, capable of learning and evolving alongside the dynamic threat landscape. These technologies enable organizations to move beyond reactive measures and embrace proactive, predictive, and responsive cybersecurity strategies. As the digital realm continues to expand, AI and ML offer a beacon of hope, empowering organizations to navigate the intricate landscape of cyber threats with resilience, agility, and the unwavering determination to safeguard their operations, data, and the trust of stakeholders.

Predictions for the future of cybersecurity

As technology advances at an unprecedented pace, reshaping industries and the very fabric of daily life, cybersecurity finds itself at a crossroads. The evolving threat landscape, fueled by the increasing complexity of digital interactions, demands a forward-looking approach to safeguarding sensitive data, critical infrastructure, and digital experiences. This section explores the predictions for the future of cybersecurity, delving into emerging trends, challenges, and opportunities that will shape the strategies, technologies, and mindset required to navigate the uncharted waters of the digital landscape.

Artificial intelligence (AI) and machine learning (ML) are poised to play a pivotal role in the future of cybersecurity. While they promise to bolster threat detection, response, and prediction, they also introduce challenges. AI-powered attacks, capable of autonomously adapting to defenses, could lead to a new era of self-evolving malware. Adversarial machine learning, where attackers manipulate AI algorithms, might undermine the integrity of AI-driven security systems. Striking the delicate balance between using AI for defense and guarding against its misuse will be a central challenge in the cybersecurity landscape.

Quantum computing's advent heralds a revolution in computing power, capable of cracking encryption algorithms that safeguard sensitive data today. While quantum encryption methods are being developed to counter this threat, the transition will require massive changes in existing cryptographic infrastructure. The race to quantum readiness—where organizations and governments prepare for quantum-based attacks—is on. The future will witness a tug-of-war between quantum computing's potential to enhance security and its capacity to undermine established cryptographic safeguards.

The shift from perimeter-based security to zero trust architecture is gaining momentum. Trust is not automatically granted based on location in this model, and access is verified for every interaction. As cloud computing, remote work, and hybrid environments become standard, zero trust will be critical in ensuring data security. A thorough understanding of the organization's digital ecosystem is necessary for the implementation and management of a zero trust framework, which is complex. The future will see a continued shift toward this security paradigm, with its success hinging on seamless integration and user-friendly experiences.

The SolarWinds incident highlighted the susceptibility of supply chains to cyber attacks. Organizations will increasingly prioritize assessing and fortifying their supply chain partners' cybersecurity measures. The future will demand comprehensive vendor risk management, with companies conducting rigorous due diligence and holding partners accountable for security standards. To ensure the overall resilience of interconnected systems, collaboration between enterprises and their supply chain partners will be crucial.

As technology advances, human psychology remains a pivotal vulnerability. Cybercriminals exploit human behavior through tactics like social engineering and phishing. Future cybersecurity strategies will prioritize human-centric security, combining technology with comprehensive training programs that educate users about the evolving tactics of cyber threats. Empowering individuals to recognize and respond to these threats will be central to fortifying the human link in the cybersecurity chain.

The global nature of cyber threats requires international cooperation and harmonized regulations. Countries will likely introduce or enhance cybersecurity regulations to safeguard critical infrastructure and personal data. The future will emphasize cross-border collaboration, information sharing, and collective defense mechanisms against cyber threats. Organizations operating across jurisdictions must navigate an evolving landscape of compliance requirements and engage in global cybersecurity initiatives.

The rise of emerging technologies—such as 5G, Internet of Things (IoT), and edge computing—brings both opportunities and challenges for cybersecurity. 5G's high-speed connectivity accelerates digital transformation and expands the attack surface. IoT's proliferation introduces more devices susceptible to compromise. Edge computing enhances data processing but can also decentralize security controls. The future of cybersecurity will revolve around integrating security into these technologies from their inception rather than retrofitting defenses afterward.

Predicting the future of cybersecurity is a venture into a landscape characterized by constant flux. As technological innovations continue to reshape industries and societies, the cyber threat landscape will evolve in tandem. Organizations and individuals alike must adopt an adaptive mindset, embracing agility, collaboration, and a relentless pursuit of innovation in defense. The future of cybersecurity requires a multidimensional approach that combines cutting-edge technologies, human-centric strategies, international cooperation, and a commitment to resilience. By charting this course, we pioneer a secure digital frontier where the promise of technological progress can be fully realized without compromising the safety and integrity of the digital ecosystem.

CHAPTER XI

Ethical Hacking
and Penetration Testing

Understanding ethical hacking and its purpose

In cybersecurity, hacking conjures images of covert activities aimed at compromising systems, stealing data, and wreaking havoc. However, a distinct and pivotal facet of hacking is ethical hacking, which stands as a force for good in the complex digital landscape. The skills of ethical hackers, also referred to as "white hat" hackers, are used to find flaws, pinpoint weaknesses, and improve the security of systems, networks, and applications. This section delves into ethical hacking, elucidating its purpose, methodologies, and its crucial role in the ongoing battle to secure the digital realm.

At its core, ethical hacking involves the controlled simulation of cyber attacks on systems, networks, and applications to identify vulnerabilities before malicious actors can exploit them. While ethical hackers harness the same techniques as their malicious counterparts, their actions are authorized and seek to benefit organizations and users. Their mandate is to expose weaknesses, provide recommendations for remediation, and ensure that digital assets remain resilient in the face of evolving threats. The distinction between ethical hacking and malicious hacking lies in intent and authorization—ethical hackers work transparently and collaboratively to enhance security.

Ethical hacking serves two purposes: safeguarding digital assets and facilitating continuous improvement in cybersecurity measures. By simulating attacks, ethical hackers identify vulnerabilities that malicious actors could exploit. Organizations can address these vulnerabilities proactively, fortifying their defenses against potential threats. The iterative cycle of testing, discovery, remediation, and reevaluation ingrained in ethical hacking drives the enhancement of security protocols and promotes a culture of vigilance and preparedness.

Ethical hackers employ a range of methodologies to simulate real-world cyber attacks and assess vulnerabilities comprehensively. Penetration testing, or "pen testing," involves exploiting vulnerabilities to gain unauthorized access, exposing potential weak points. Vulnerability assessment involves scanning networks, systems, and applications to identify known vulnerabilities. Web application testing assesses the security of web-based platforms, identifying vulnerabilities like SQL injection or cross-site scripting. Wireless network testing evaluates the security of Wi-Fi networks. Social engineering assessments gauge an organization's susceptibility to manipulation tactics. Each methodology contributes to a holistic evaluation of an organization's security posture.

Ethical hacking is guided by certifications and frameworks that establish best practices, methodologies, and ethical considerations. Certifications like Certified Ethical Hacker (CEH) and Offensive Security Certified Professional (OSCP) validate the skills and knowledge of ethical hackers. Frameworks, like the NIST Cybersecurity Framework and OWASP Top Ten, provide guidelines for assessing and mitigating vulnerabilities. Adhering to these certifications and frameworks ensures that ethical hackers operate within ethical and legal boundaries, emphasizing the importance of responsible hacking practices.

With the promise of financial rewards, bug bounty programs have become popular ways to encourage ethical hackers to find vulnerabilities. Organizations offer bounties for discovering security flaws, motivating a global community of skilled hackers to contribute to their cybersecurity efforts. These programs promote cooperation, encourage responsible disclosure, and make better use of the collective cybersecurity community's expertise.

Ethical hacking emerges as a steadfast ally in the ongoing battle for digital resilience in a rapidly evolving digital landscape marked by relentless cyber threats. Its purpose transcends traditional security measures, focusing on proactively identifying and mitigating vulnerabilities before they can be exploited for malicious intent. Ethical hackers forge stronger digital defenses by exposing weaknesses, enhancing security protocols, and contributing to a culture of cybersecurity awareness. They stand as sentinels who embrace the hacker mindset for the greater good—a testament to the intricate dance between offense and protection in the quest to safeguard the integrity, privacy, and trust that underpin our interconnected digital world.

Importance of penetration testing for identifying vulnerabilities

In the relentless battle against cyber threats, where organizations face constantly evolving attacks, penetration testing is a critical line of defense. Penetration testing, often called "pen testing," involves simulated cyber attacks on systems, networks, and applications to identify vulnerabilities before malicious actors exploit them. This proactive approach to cybersecurity plays a pivotal role in bolstering digital fortresses by revealing weaknesses, enabling organizations to patch vulnerabilities, and ensuring the resilience of their digital assets. This section delves into the significance of penetration testing, exploring its methodologies, benefits, and role in fortifying the modern digital landscape.

The digital ecosystem is rife with known and unknown vulnerabilities waiting to be exploited by cybercriminals. Penetration testing is a beacon that illuminates these hidden weaknesses before malicious actors discover them. By simulating real-world attacks, ethical hackers replicate the tactics and techniques used by cybercriminals to infiltrate systems and gain unauthorized access. This process unearths vulnerabilities that might not have been apparent through conventional security assessments. Organizations can then address these vulnerabilities proactively, reducing the potential for successful cyber attacks and minimizing the associated risks.

Penetration testing encompasses a wide range of methodologies that evaluate an organization's security posture from various angles. External penetration testing assesses the security of internet-facing systems, simulating attacks from external actors. Internal penetration testing evaluates the security measures within an organization's internal network. Web application testing focuses on web-based platforms, identifying vulnerabilities that could be exploited through web interfaces. Wireless network testing gauges the security of Wi-Fi networks, while social engineering assessments assess human vulnerabilities. This comprehensive approach ensures that vulnerabilities are identified across the entirety of an organization's digital landscape.

The authenticity of penetration testing lies in its ability to replicate the tactics and techniques employed by actual cybercriminals. This realism ensures that vulnerabilities identified through testing accurately mirror the threats organizations face in the real world. Whether it's exploiting software vulnerabilities, social engineering tactics, or attempting to breach perimeter defenses, penetration testing provides insights into the ways in which attackers might compromise systems. This information enables organizations to take targeted and strategic measures to strengthen their defenses.

The cost of a cyber attack extends beyond financial implications—it encompasses reputational damage, legal consequences, and operational disruptions. Penetration testing is a proactive investment in risk management, as it enables organizations to identify vulnerabilities and address them before they are exploited. The financial outlay for penetration testing pales compared to the potential costs of a data breach or a compromised system. By preventing breaches, organizations avoid the financial and reputational fallout that can arise from a successful cyber attack.

In an era of heightened cybersecurity regulations and data protection laws, penetration testing is crucial in ensuring compliance. Many industries require organizations to meet specific cybersecurity standards and demonstrate their commitment to safeguarding data. Penetration testing provides evidence of due diligence and adherence to industry regulations. Moreover, organizations that regularly conduct penetration testing showcase their commitment to cybersecurity to customers, partners, and stakeholders, fostering trust in their digital operations.

The evolving cyber threat scenario necessitates constant development of cybersecurity measures. Penetration testing is not a one-time endeavor; rather, it should be an ongoing practice that aligns with the pace of evolving threats. Regular testing allows organizations to track their progress in addressing vulnerabilities, adapt to emerging attack vectors, and refine their incident response strategies. This iterative cycle of testing, remediating, and reevaluating ensures that an organization's digital defenses remain robust and resilient in the face of ever-changing cyber threats.

In an era of digital transformation, organizations cannot afford to be passive observers in the battle against cyber threats. Penetration testing offers a proactive and strategic approach to fortifying digital defenses, enabling organizations to identify vulnerabilities, assess risks, and remediate weaknesses before they are exploited. By mimicking the tactics of cybercriminals and uncovering hidden vulnerabilities, penetration testing serves as a crucible for refining cybersecurity measures. Its role extends beyond risk management; it fosters a culture of vigilance, trust, and continuous improvement in the digital realm. As organizations navigate the complexities of the modern threat landscape, penetration testing is a cornerstone in safeguarding their digital assets and upholding the integrity, privacy, and trust that define our interconnected world.

How to start an ethical hacking career

In a world where the digital landscape continually evolves and cyber threats loom ever more significant, the role of ethical hackers has become paramount in safeguarding the integrity of digital ecosystems. The protectors of cybersecurity are ethical hackers, commonly referred to as "white hat" hackers. They use their knowledge to spot vulnerabilities, safeguard systems, and outwit malicious actors. For those drawn to the exhilarating challenge of outthinking cybercriminals and fortifying digital defenses, a career in ethical hacking offers an exciting and rewarding path. This section delves into the journey of becoming an ethical hacker, exploring the requisite skills, educational pathways, certifications, and the significance of ethical hacking in the modern cybersecurity landscape.

Ethical hacking demands a diverse skill set that combines technical prowess, critical thinking, and a hacker's mindset for problem-solving. It is essential to be proficient in programming languages including Python, Java, and C++ and to have a thorough understanding of operating systems, networking protocols, and database administration. Familiarity with security tools, such as penetration testing frameworks and vulnerability scanners, is essential for uncovering and addressing vulnerabilities. Effective communication skills are equally vital, enabling ethical hackers to convey complex technical concepts to non-technical stakeholders and collaborate with interdisciplinary teams.

While ethical hacking is a skill-intensive field, a solid educational foundation is crucial for success. Many ethical hackers possess computer science, information technology, or cybersecurity degrees. These programs provide a comprehensive understanding of computer systems, networks, and security principles. However, formal education is just the beginning—ethical hackers often engage in continuous self-learning to keep pace with the rapidly evolving cyber threat landscape.

Certifications are pivotal in demonstrating expertise and credibility in ethical hacking. The Certified Ethical Hacker (CEH) certification is one of the industry's most recognized and sought-after certifications. It covers topics ranging from network security and penetration testing to cryptography and web application security. Similarly, the CompTIA Security+ certification provides a foundational understanding of cybersecurity concepts. For those seeking advanced knowledge, the Offensive Security Certified Professional (OSCP) certification challenges candidates with a rigorous hands-on exam that assesses their penetration testing skills.

Hands-on experience is the crucible where theoretical knowledge meets practical application. Aspiring ethical hackers can set up virtual labs to practice various techniques in a controlled environment. Engaging in Capture The Flag (CTF) competitions, where participants solve cybersecurity challenges, hone problem-solving skills and expose individuals to various scenarios. Internships, apprenticeships, or entry-level positions in cybersecurity also offer valuable real-world experience, allowing individuals to work alongside seasoned professionals and apply their skills in a professional setting.

Ethical hacking extends beyond technical skills—it embodies a hacker ethos characterized by curiosity, creativity, and a commitment to learning. Ethical hackers possess an insatiable appetite for uncovering how systems work, identifying vulnerabilities, and pushing the boundaries of their knowledge. This mindset fosters innovation, adaptability, and resilience—indispensable qualities in the ever-changing cybersecurity landscape.

In an era of digital transformation and rising cyberthreats, the value of ethical hacking cannot be overemphasized. Ethical hackers play a pivotal role in identifying vulnerabilities before malicious actors can exploit them, protecting sensitive data, critical infrastructure, and digital experiences. They collaborate with organizations to enhance cybersecurity measures, thwart cyber attacks, and ensure the integrity of digital ecosystems. The ethical hacking community embodies the principle that knowledge is power—and with great power comes great responsibility.

As the digital realm expands its influence across every facet of modern life, the need for ethical hackers has never been greater. Pursuing a career in ethical hacking requires dedication, continuous learning, and a commitment to ethical conduct. The journey involves building technical expertise, obtaining certifications, gaining hands-on experience, and embracing the hacker ethos. Ethical hackers are the defenders of the digital frontier, equipped with the skills to outsmart cybercriminals and safeguard the interconnected world we rely upon. Their contributions help to shape cybersecurity's future and pave the way for a digital environment that is both safer and more robust. For those who embark on this journey, the realm of ethical hacking offers a challenging and rewarding career and the opportunity to be the vanguard of digital defenders in an ever-evolving cyber battleground.

CHAPTER XII

Staying Informed and Cyber Aware

Resources for staying up-to-date on cybersecurity news

In the ever-shifting landscape of cybersecurity, staying informed about the latest threats, trends, and best practices is not just a choice—it's a necessity. As cyber attacks become more sophisticated and pervasive, individuals and organizations must remain vigilant and adaptable to safeguard their digital assets. Fortunately, a wealth of resources exists to provide timely and relevant cybersecurity news, insights, and analysis. This section delves into the diverse resources available for staying up-to-date on cybersecurity news, from reputable news outlets and industry-specific publications to online communities, podcasts, and specialized blogs.

Established news outlets are pivotal in delivering accurate and comprehensive cybersecurity news. Sources like The New York Times, Reuters, and The Wall Street Journal often cover major cyber incidents, policy developments, and industry trends. These outlets provide a broader context for understanding the intersection of technology, security, and society. Their comprehensive coverage ensures that individuals and professionals are informed about the broader implications of cybersecurity events.

For more targeted and in-depth coverage, industry-specific publications are invaluable resources. Magazines like SC Magazine and Dark Reading offer a wealth of articles, features, and analyses focusing solely on cybersecurity. These sources delve into topics such as threat intelligence, best practices, emerging technologies, and regulatory updates. Industry-specific publications provide a deep dive into the nuances of cybersecurity, catering to the needs of professionals seeking specialized knowledge.

Online communities and forums bring together cybersecurity enthusiasts, professionals, and experts to share insights, discuss recent developments, and seek advice. Platforms like Reddit's r/netsec, Hacker News, and specialized forums such as BleepingComputer foster discussions on current threats, vulnerabilities, and incident response strategies. Engaging with these communities offers diverse perspectives and provides real-world anecdotes and experiences from those on the front lines of cybersecurity.

Podcasts offer a convenient way to consume cybersecurity news and insights while on the move. Shows like "Security Now," "CyberWire," and "Risky Business" feature interviews with industry experts, discussions on recent breaches, and analysis of emerging threats. Podcasts provide a dynamic and engaging format for staying informed, offering listeners the chance to learn from experts and thought leaders in the field.

Blogs authored by cybersecurity professionals, researchers, and thought leaders offer unique perspectives and deep dives into specific cybersecurity topics. Blogs like Schneier on Security by Bruce Schneier and Krebs on Security by Brian Krebs provide expert analyses, investigative reporting, and thought-provoking commentary on current cybersecurity issues. Following these blogs offers insights into cutting-edge research, new attack techniques, and countermeasures.

Threat intelligence platforms deliver real-time updates on emerging threats, vulnerabilities, and attack campaigns. Services like ThreatConnect and Recorded Future compile and analyze data from numerous sources to deliver useful threat intelligence. Subscribing to these platforms equips individuals and organizations with up-to-the-minute information on evolving threat landscapes.

Many cybersecurity solution providers maintain blogs and newsletters that offer insights from the front lines of defense. These resources provide information about new vulnerabilities, patches, and security best practices. Subscribing to vendor newsletters informs users about the latest tools, technologies, and strategies for protecting digital assets.

Social media sites including LinkedIn and Twitter serve as hubs for discussions, news, and updates related to cybersecurity. Following reputable cybersecurity experts, organizations, and news outlets on these platforms provides a steady stream of information. Moreover, participating in relevant LinkedIn groups and Twitter chats fosters engagement, knowledge-sharing, and networking within the cybersecurity community.

Cybersecurity conferences and webinars offer a chance to learn from industry leaders, researchers, and practitioners. While in-person events provide networking opportunities, virtual conferences and webinars have become increasingly popular due to their accessibility. Events like Black Hat, DEFCON, and RSA Conference offer presentations, panels, and discussions on the latest cybersecurity trends.

Staying up-to-date on cybersecurity news is not a passive endeavor—it's an ongoing commitment to learning, adaptation, and vigilance. The diverse resources available—reputable news outlets, industry publications, online communities, podcasts, blogs, threat intelligence platforms, vendor blogs, social media, and professional networks—offer a multifaceted approach to staying informed. By tapping into these resources, individuals and organizations navigate the deluge of cybersecurity information, gaining insights into emerging threats, evolving attack techniques, and innovative defense strategies. In the ever-changing realm of cybersecurity, knowledge is the most potent shield against digital threats, enabling us to confidently safeguard our digital fortresses and navigate the complexities of the interconnected world.

Building a cybersecurity mindset for daily digital activities

Our daily activities seamlessly integrate with the digital realm in an era characterized by digital interconnectedness. From personal communications to financial transactions, technology is becoming increasingly ingrained in our daily lives. However, this integration also exposes us to various cyber threats, from phishing attacks to data breaches. To navigate the digital frontier safely, cultivating a cybersecurity mindset is essential. This mindset goes beyond passwords and firewalls; it encompasses a holistic approach to digital hygiene, awareness, and proactive defense. This section explores the significance of building a cybersecurity mindset for daily digital activities, highlighting fundamental principles and practices that empower individuals to protect their digital lives.

A cybersecurity mindset begins with understanding the evolving cyber threat landscape. Awareness of common threats such as phishing, malware, and social engineering empowers individuals to recognize and respond effectively. Staying informed about recent breaches, vulnerabilities, and emerging attack vectors provides valuable insights into the tactics used by cybercriminals. Regularly accessing reputable cybersecurity news and insights sources enables individuals to remain informed about the latest trends and stay one step ahead of potential threats.

Digital hygiene forms the bedrock of a cybersecurity mindset. Simple practices, such as keeping software up to date, regularly changing passwords, and using strong, unique passwords for each account, prevent unauthorized access. A further layer of security is added by enabling multi-factor authentication. Important practices that reduce risks include avoiding using public Wi-Fi for important transactions and avoiding clicking on suspicious URLs or downloading attachments from unknown sources.

A cybersecurity mindset is rooted in critical thinking and vigilance. Individuals should question the request's legitimacy before clicking on links, downloading files, or sharing personal information. Scrutinizing email sender addresses and the content of messages can reveal subtle signs of phishing attempts. Applying the principle of "think before you click" cultivates a habit of skepticism, reducing the likelihood of falling victim to social engineering tactics.

Protecting personal data is paramount in a cybersecurity mindset. Limiting the information shared on social media platforms and adjusting privacy settings ensures that sensitive details are not readily accessible to potential attackers. Additionally, understanding how organizations handle personal data and reading privacy policies before sharing information online enhances awareness of data security practices.

A cybersecurity mindset extends beyond personal practices—it involves educating and empowering others. Sharing knowledge about cybersecurity best practices with friends, family, and colleagues fosters a culture of awareness. Educating the next generation about responsible online behavior equips them to navigate the digital landscape safely. Individuals contribute to a collective effort to enhance digital resilience by promoting cybersecurity principles.

The development of Internet of Things (IoT) devices makes the cybersecurity environment more complicated. A robust cybersecurity mindset includes securing these devices, such as smart home appliances and wearable gadgets. Changing default passwords, updating firmware, and configuring devices to limit their exposure to potential vulnerabilities are essential steps in safeguarding the broader digital ecosystem.

A cybersecurity mindset is dynamic—it evolves with the threat landscape. New attack vectors emerge, and cyber criminals continuously adapt their tactics. Engaging in continuous learning through online courses, webinars, and cybersecurity communities equips individuals with the knowledge to counter new threats. Embracing a constant vigilance and adaptability mindset ensures that individuals are well-prepared to respond to evolving challenges.

In an era where technology is an integral part of our lives, building a cybersecurity mindset is not a luxury—it's a necessity. This way of thinking gives individuals the power to take charge of their online interactions, guaranteeing that they may reap the rewards of technology without being exposed to its risks. It's a mindset that prioritizes knowledge, critical thinking, and proactive defense. By cultivating this mindset, individuals become empowered digital citizens who confidently navigate the complexities of the digital age, safeguarding their personal information, financial assets, and online interactions. With each informed decision and security-conscious action, they contribute to a safer and more resilient digital ecosystem for themselves and future generations.

Promoting cybersecurity awareness in your community

In an increasingly interconnected world, the need for cybersecurity awareness has transcended individual responsibility—it has become a collective imperative. Cyber threats, ranging from identity theft to ransomware attacks, can impact individuals, families, and communities at large. Promoting cybersecurity awareness within your community is not just about safeguarding personal data; it's about fostering a culture of digital resilience that protects everyone. This section delves into the importance of promoting cybersecurity awareness in your community, highlighting strategies, initiatives, and the far-reaching impact of a united front against cyber threats.

Cyber threats don't discriminate—they can affect anyone, irrespective of age, profession, or background. When individuals within a community are equipped with cybersecurity knowledge, their ability to protect themselves and their families increases. Furthermore, a community armed with cybersecurity awareness can collectively thwart potential attacks that target multiple individuals or organizations. By recognizing the interconnectedness of digital lives, promoting cybersecurity awareness empowers everyone to contribute to a safer online environment.

The cornerstone of promoting cybersecurity awareness is education. Organizing workshops, webinars, and seminars that address cybersecurity basics—ranging from password hygiene to recognizing phishing attempts—imparts valuable knowledge. These educational sessions should cater to different age groups, adapting the content to suit the needs and concerns of children, parents, and seniors. Collaborating with local schools, community centers, and libraries offers accessible venues for disseminating cybersecurity information.

Engaging with local organizations magnifies the impact of cybersecurity awareness initiatives. Partnering with schools, libraries, neighborhood associations, and business chambers allows for a wider reach. These collaborations can involve hosting joint events, distributing educational materials, and conducting interactive sessions on cybersecurity. Community-wide efforts are more effective in disseminating essential cybersecurity information by pooling resources and expertise.

Children's online conduct is significantly shaped by parents and guardians. Organizing workshops that equip parents with the knowledge to guide their children's digital activities ensures a multi-generational approach to cybersecurity awareness. Empowering parents to set parental controls, monitor online interactions, and educate their children about the risks of sharing personal information online creates a safer digital environment for young community members.

Different communities have distinct needs and concerns when it comes to cybersecurity. Urban areas might focus on online financial safety and identity theft prevention, while rural communities might prioritize cybersecurity for agricultural technologies. Tailoring awareness initiatives to address community-specific challenges ensures relevance and resonates with individuals' immediate concerns.

Social media platforms and community websites offer valuable channels for promoting cybersecurity awareness. Sharing informative articles, infographics, and videos on these platforms disseminates knowledge to a broad audience. Hosting virtual events, Q&A sessions, and interactive challenges encourages engagement and provides a space for individuals to ask questions and share experiences.

Promoting cybersecurity awareness is not solely about information dissemination; it's about modeling good practices. Demonstrating strong password management, using multi-factor authentication, and exercising caution while clicking on links sets an example for others to follow. When community members witness responsible digital behavior in action, it encourages them to adopt similar practices.

Encouraging community members to report suspicious online activities fosters a proactive approach to cybersecurity. Clear reporting channels for cyber incidents, whether through community websites, regional law enforcement, or cybersecurity organizations, guarantee that potential threats are found and promptly addressed. Promoting a culture of reporting diminishes the stigma associated with falling victim to cyber attacks and empowers individuals to seek help when needed.

October is recognized as National Cybersecurity Awareness Month in many countries. Leveraging this dedicated month to organize special events, campaigns, and initiatives amplifies cybersecurity awareness efforts. Collaborating with local media, schools, businesses, and community centers to spread the word about cybersecurity during this month creates a more significant impact and resonates with a broader audience.

Promoting cybersecurity awareness in your community is more than a mission—it's a movement. By educating, engaging, and empowering individuals of all ages and backgrounds, you contribute to a united front against cyber threats. This collective effort not only safeguards personal data but also reinforces the digital resilience of your community. Each individual's commitment to adopting cybersecurity best practices ripples through families, neighborhoods, and organizations, creating a safer online environment for everyone. Promoting cybersecurity awareness is an investment in a digitally secure future where empowered digital defenders stand resilient against the ever-evolving landscape of cyber threats.

CONCLUSION

Recap of key cybersecurity concepts covered in the e-book

Throughout this e-book, we've embarked on a journey through cybersecurity, uncovering essential concepts that empower individuals to safeguard their digital lives. From understanding the foundations of cybersecurity to navigating the complex landscape of threats and defenses, we've delved into various topics that collectively form the pillars of digital resilience.

We began by defining cybersecurity and highlighting its significance in an increasingly digital world. We explored the myriad types of cyber threats, from malware and phishing to hacking and social engineering, dissecting their tactics and shedding light on cybercriminals' methods to compromise digital security.

Our exploration extended to identifying common vulnerabilities within digital systems. We analyzed the weaknesses that attackers exploit and underscored the importance of shoring up these vulnerabilities to prevent breaches. Moreover, we delved into an in-depth exploration of different types of cyber attacks, unveiling the intricacies of DDoS attacks, ransomware incidents, and more.

Real-world examples of major cyber attacks painted a vivid picture of the potential consequences of inadequate cybersecurity measures. From the NotPetya ransomware attack to the Equifax data breach, these incidents demonstrated the far-reaching impacts of cyber threats on individuals, organizations, and even national security.

Digging deeper, we explored the motivations driving cyber attacks—financial gain, espionage, activism—and dissected the psychology behind these motives. This understanding illuminated the multifaceted cybercrime landscape, where profit, ideology, and geopolitical tensions intersect.

Strong passwords and effective password management emerged as a critical aspect of personal cybersecurity. We uncovered the techniques to craft secure passwords and the significance of employing unique credentials across various accounts.

Multi-factor authentication (MFA) emerged as a vital tool in identity protection, acting as a formidable barrier against unauthorized access. We explored its role in thwarting cybercriminals and providing an additional layer of defense in an interconnected world.

The risks of public Wi-Fi and strategies for its safe usage were revealed, emphasizing the importance of cautious connectivity in an era where public networks are ubiquitous and vulnerable.

Safeguarding sensitive files and data became paramount as we explored encryption, secure file storage, and data protection techniques to shield personal and sensitive information from prying eyes.

Cloud storage security was demystified, highlighting the significance of encryption and secure practices when storing data in the cloud. The importance of regular backups underscored the need to preserve data integrity and accessibility.

We navigated the intricate terrain of social engineering tactics, uncovering the manipulation techniques used by cybercriminals to exploit human vulnerabilities. This exploration offered insights into recognizing and countering these subtle yet powerful methods.

We delved into the realm of ethical hacking, discussing its purpose, significance, and the practice of penetration testing as a means of identifying vulnerabilities and fortifying digital defenses.

The essay revealed the role of artificial intelligence and machine learning in bolstering cybersecurity measures and predicting the future of cyber threats. Our journey culminated with a comprehensive exploration of strategies to foster cybersecurity awareness in communities, empowering individuals to take a collective stand against cyber threats.

As we conclude this e-book, armed with a holistic understanding of cybersecurity essentials, we stand prepared to navigate the digital world with vigilance, awareness, and resilience. The principles, insights, and practices gleaned from these pages provide a roadmap to fortifying our digital fortresses, ensuring that our interactions, transactions, and digital experiences are underpinned by security, trust, and a steadfast commitment to safeguarding our interconnected lives.

Encouragement to take proactive steps in safeguarding digital life

In the ever-expanding landscape of the digital world, the onus of safeguarding our online existence falls squarely on our shoulders. The threats are real, the consequences profound, but so too is our ability to take proactive measures that shield us from the perils that lurk in the virtual shadows. It's not a matter of if, but when our digital footprints intersect with cyber threats—and in that pivotal moment, our actions to fortify our digital defenses will determine our fate.

To embrace the role of a digital defender, the first step is awareness. We must recognize that the world we navigate today is a blend of physical and virtual realms, where our emails, photos, financial transactions, and even our thoughts find a home in the vast expanse of cyberspace. With this awareness comes the understanding that every click, every download, and every interaction can either be a point of vulnerability or a beacon of security.

From awareness, we transition to action. Crafting strong and unique passwords, embracing multi-factor authentication, and updating software are not mere suggestions; they are the building blocks of digital resilience. Proactivity means engaging with privacy settings on social media platforms, encrypting sensitive files, and staying vigilant against phishing attempts. It means educating ourselves about the latest threats and trends in cybersecurity because knowledge is the most potent armor we possess.

Embracing proactive cybersecurity measures doesn't stop at the individual level—it extends to our families, friends, and communities. As proudly as we educate our loved ones to cross the street looking both ways, we should equally stress the need of carefully reading emails, spotting suspicious links, and respecting the confidentiality of personal information. By fostering a culture of cybersecurity awareness, we create a ripple effect that fortifies the digital lives of those around us.

Moreover, proactivity involves holding organizations accountable for the protection of our data. We should demand transparency about storing, using, and safeguarding our information. As consumers, we can choose service providers prioritizing security and respecting privacy. Our decisions convey that cybersecurity is not negotiable—it's a fundamental expectation.

The journey of digital safeguarding is ongoing as the threat landscape continually evolves. However, this should not deter us. Instead, it should empower us to embrace a lifelong commitment to learning, adapting, and fortifying our defenses. We should remain curious, interested, and willing to explore new tools and technologies that enhance our security posture.

As we navigate the intricacies of the digital world, let us remember that the power to protect ourselves is within reach. We bolster our digital resilience with each proactive step we take—whether it's setting up multi-factor authentication, teaching our children about online safety, or championing cybersecurity awareness in our communities. In a world where our lives are increasingly shaped by technology, the ability to protect what matters most is a responsibility that belongs to each of us. We can ensure a more secure and safer digital future for ourselves and generations to come by taking proactive measures today.

Final thoughts on the ever-evolving nature of cybersecurity

In the realm of cybersecurity, the only constant is change. As we conclude this exploration of the multifaceted world of digital defense, it's imperative to reflect on the ever-evolving nature of cybersecurity—a landscape defined by innovation, adaptation, and the perpetual dance between defenders and adversaries.

The digital landscape is continually changing due to the quick pace of technological development, which is also creating new opportunities for comfort, connectivity, and creativity. Yet, with each advancement, a parallel challenge arises: the quest to secure these innovations against increasingly sophisticated cyber threats. Just as our lives are enriched by technology, our vulnerabilities also multiply.

The nature of cyber threats is fluid, evolving in tandem with the technologies they exploit. Attackers are adept at adapting their tactics, targeting new vulnerabilities, and using the weakest links in our digital armor. To thrive in this landscape, defenders must cultivate a mindset of constant vigilance, staying attuned to emerging threats and arming themselves with the latest insights and techniques.

In this dynamic dance between defenders and adversaries, the role of collaboration cannot be overstated. Just as cybercriminals form networks to share tactics and tools, defenders must unite to pool their expertise and insights. The cybersecurity community is a force of resilience—a collective defense that spans industries, borders, and ideologies. The power of this community lies not just in its technical prowess but in its shared commitment to safeguarding the digital realm.

The legacy of innovation offers both promise and peril. As artificial intelligence and the Internet of Things become woven into our lives fabric, they offer new ways for cybercriminals to exploit vulnerabilities. However, they also provide defenders with potent tools to predict, detect, and counteract threats. This duality underscores the need for a proactive approach that anticipates challenges and harnesses innovation to outpace adversaries.

As we traverse this landscape, it's crucial to acknowledge that cybersecurity is not a destination but a journey. It's a journey that requires us to shed complacency, embrace a culture of continuous learning, and cultivate resilience in the face of adversity. It's a journey that transcends the individual and extends to families, communities, organizations, and societies.

The stories of major cyber attacks remind us that the impact of cybersecurity breaches extends far beyond code and data. It impacts trust, economic stability, and even national security. Each incident underscores the gravity of our collective responsibility. Every line of code, every security measure, and every informed decision contributes to a safer digital world.

Let's keep in mind that every action we take have an impact on society's digital infrastructure as we navigate the constantly changing terrain of cybersecurity. The choices we make today shape the future for ourselves, our children, and the generations to come. The commitment to cybersecurity is a commitment to a safer, more connected, and more resilient world. It's a commitment to fostering innovation without forsaking security and embracing the challenges of the digital age with unwavering resolve.

In this final reflection, we stand as digital defenders, united by a shared mission. Let us face the unknown with curiosity, meet challenges with resilience, and champion the cause of cybersecurity awareness. As we bid farewell to these pages, let our collective journey continue—a journey marked by vigilance, empowerment, and a steadfast determination to safeguard the digital landscape for a brighter future.

Thank you for buying and reading/listening to our book. If you found this book useful/helpful please take a few minutes and leave a review on the platform where you purchased our book. Your feedback matters greatly to us.